MELAB® Test Strategy

Winning Multiple Choice Strategies for the Michigan English Language Arts Battery

Published by

Complete TEST Preparation Inc.

Copyright © 2011 by Brian Stocker. ALL RIGHTS RESERVED. No part of this book may be reproduced or transferred in any form or by any means, graphic, electronic, or mechanical, including photocopying, recording, web distribution, taping, or by any information storage retrieval system, without the written permission of the author.

Notice: Complete Test Preparation makes every reasonable effort to obtain from reliable sources accurate, complete, and timely information about the tests covered in this book. Nevertheless, changes can be made in the tests or the administration of the tests at any time and Complete Test Preparation makes no representation or warranty, either expressed or implied as the accuracy, timeliness, or completeness of the information contained in this book. Complete Test Preparation make no representations or warranties of any kind, express or implied, about the completeness, accuracy, reliability, suitability or availability with respect to the information contained in this document for any purpose. Any reliance you place on such information is therefore strictly at your own risk.

The author(s) shall not be liable for any loss incurred as a consequence of the use and application, directly or indirectly, of any information presented in this work. Sold with the understanding, the author is not engaged in rendering professional services or advice. If advice or expert assistance is required, the services of a competent professional should be sought.

The company, product and service names used in this publication are for identification purposes only. All trademarks and registered trademarks are the property of their respective owners. Complete Test Preparation is not affiliated with any educational institution.

We strongly recommend that students check with exam providers for up-to-date information regarding test content.

MELAB® is a registered trademark of Cambridge Michigan Language Assessment LLC, who are not involved in the production of, and do not endorse this product.

ISBN-13: 9781772452099

Version 6.6 August 2016
Published by
Complete Test Preparation Inc.

Victoria BC Canada
Visit us on the web at http://www.test-preparation.ca
Printed in the USA

About Complete Test Preparation Inc.

The Complete Test Preparation Team has been publishing high quality study materials since 2005. Millions of students visit our websites every year, and thousands of students, teachers and parents all over the world have purchased our teaching materials, curriculum, study guides and practice tests.

Complete Test Preparation is committed to providing students with the best study materials and practice tests available on the market. Members of our team combine years of teaching experience, with experienced writers and editors, all with advanced degrees (Masters or higher).

Visit us on the web at http://www.test-preparation.ca

Contents

7 Getting Started with the MELAB®
  Test Strategy — 8

9 Answering Multiple Choice
  A Better Score Is Possible — 9
  Tips for Reading the Instructions — 12
  General Multiple Choice Tips — 14
  Answering Step-by-Step — 16

18 Multiple Choice Strategy
  Strategy Practice Questions — 20
  Answers Key — 39
  Reading Comprehension Practice — 51
  Answer Key — 64

77 English Grammar and Usage
  English Grammar Multiple Choice — 77
  Common English Usage Mistakes — 93
  Subject Verb Agreement — 99
  English Grammar Practice Questions — 106
  Answer Key — 117

124 How to Improve your Vocabulary
  Meaning in Context — 129
  Answer Key — 139
  Top 100 Common Vocabulary — 143
  Stem Words — 147
  Stem Words Practice Questions I — 166
  Answer Key — 177
  Stem Words Practice II — 182
  Answer Key — 192
  Most Common Prefix — 197
  Prefix Questions Part I — 203
  Answer Key — 208
  Prefix Questions Part II — 210
  Answer Key — 215
  Most Common Synonyms — 217
  Synonym Practice Questions — 222
  Answer Key — 229

	Most Common Antonyms	232
	Antonym Practice Questions	237
	Answer Key	243

246 How to Prepare for a Test
Mental Prep 248

251 How to Take a Test
How to Take a Test - The Basics 252
In the Test Room 256
Avoid Anxiety Prior to a Test 261
Common Test-Taking Mistakes 263

265 Conclusion

Getting Started with the MELAB®

CONGRATULATIONS! By deciding to take the Michigan English Language Arts Battery (MELAB®) you have taken the first step toward a great future! Of course, there is no point in taking this important examination unless you intend to do your best to earn the highest grade you possibly can. That means getting yourself organized and discovering the best approaches, methods and strategies to master the material. Yes, that will require real effort and dedication on your part but if you are willing to focus your energy and devote the study time necessary, before you know it you will be finished the exam with a great mark!

We know that taking on a new endeavour can be a little scary, and it is easy to feel unsure of where to begin. That's where we come in. This study guide is designed to help you improve your test-taking skills, show you a few tricks and increase both your competency and confidence.

What is on the MELAB®

The MELAB® has these sections: English grammar and Usage, Reading Comprehension, Essay, Vocabulary, Cloze, Listening Comprehension and an Oral Exam.

English – covers conversational grammar and English usage (30 questions).

Reading Comprehension – Four to five short passages are supplied with four to five multiple choice questions for each passage (20 - 30 questions).

Essay – write a short essay. Two topics are supplied.

Vocabulary – multiple choice vocabulary questions in two formats – vocabulary sentence completion, or meaning from context, and synonym substitution (25 – 30 questions).

Cloze – Fill in the blanks from a passage (15 – 20 questions).

Test Strategy

This is a book about improving your score by using proven test strategies. This is a little different from other books such as a study guide, or a practice test. Even though we do provide lots of information to study and practice test questions, this book is about how to tackle multiple choice questions.

But do not worry - that is not all! While you are learning different strategies for answering multiple choice questions, you can also practice your skill at answering reading comprehension test questions English grammar and usage, and basic math, which are half your score on the MELAB.

Answering Multiple Choice

A Better Score Is Possible

Worried about that big exam coming up? Do you think you're just not a good test-taker, especially when it comes to standardized tests? The good news is that you're not alone. The bad news is that millions of people are left behind through objective testing, simply because they're not good test-takers - even though they may know the material. They don't know how to handle the format well or understand what's expected of them.

This is especially true of the multiple-choice test. Test-takers are given lots of support for taking essay-style tests. They're helped with skills such as grammar and spelling. However, little is offered for the multiple-choice exam. This is despite the fact that thousands of people find multiple-choice to be the most challenging kind of test. Here are some reasons that so many people have difficulties with multiple-choice:

>**The Broad Range.** Because the questions are so short and quick, a lot of ground is covered in the test. Who's to know what to study with so much material covered?
>
>**Time Limits.** Most standardized tests have time limits, which adds an extra layer of pressure.
>
>**Trickery.** Many test-designers think that it is too easy to guess a multiple-choice question correctly, so they intentionally make the questions tricky.
>
>**Bluffing Not Allowed**. With an essay test, you can try to bluff your way through it. Not so with multiple-choice. The answer is either right or wrong.
>
>**Difficult to Write.** It's not easy for a test-writer to design a good multiple-choice test. Because of this, sometimes, they make them overly difficult.

Shuffled Content. Multiple-choice tests tend to throw the questions in at random, in no particular order. You could be answering a question about the 1700s and then about the 2004 Presidential election.

These challenges mean that students have to be familiar with a wider range of material than on other kinds of exams. You'll need to know specific vocabulary, rules, names, dates, etc.

There are, however, a few advantages to you, the test-taker, with a multiple-choice test. For instance, because there are more multiple-choice items on a test than there are other types, each question tends to have a lower point value. You can afford to miss a few and still be okay. Also, if you're doing a fill-in-the blank or essay test, you have to rely totally on memory for the answer. With a multiple-choice exam, you know that the correct answer is somewhere in the question. You just have to decide which one it is. Often, seeing the right answer will trigger your memory, and you'll recognize it instantly.

Keep in mind, though, the test-writer knows that one of the advantages of multiple-choice is the fact the answer is on the page. This leads to many test-writers to include what is called a "distracter." This is a possible answer that is designed to look like the correct answer, but which is actually wrong. We'll talk about this again later, but an example would be the question: "Who is known for posting 95 theses on a church wall?" Among the answers might be Martin Luther and Martin Luther King. Because the student vaguely remembers the name "Martin Luther" from the course materials, there's a chance that he'll select the incorrect "Martin Luther King."

Who Does Well On Multiple-Choice Exams?

With so many challenges working against you on the multiple-choice exam, what's the answer? Is there a way to improve your chances and your score? There is! The point of this book is not to discourage you, but to make you aware that there are strategies and tips that you can incorporate to raise your test score. Before we get into the specific strategies, let's take a general look at who does best on these types of tests.

Those who know the material. This should go without saying, but the thing that will most raise your test score will be if you know the material that's going to be covered. While the strategies we'll discuss later will help you even with questions you're unsure of, the surest thing you can do is learn the rules, dates, names, and concepts that you'll be tested on.

Those who have a calm, cool demeanor when taking a test. Panicking can cause you to forget the information you think you know. Confidence goes a long way toward a better mark on multiple-choice.

Those who meditate or pray before the test. Don't laugh. It's a known fact that people who meditate or pray, depending on their beliefs, enter a test room more confidently, and do better on the exam.

Those who operate on logic rather than instinct. Those who take a multiple-choice test based on instinct will be tempted to overlook the stated facts, and let emotion rule.

Those who have a system. Most of the book will deal with this, but you should not just guess randomly on questions you don't know. You must have a systematic strategy.

Types of Multiple-Choice Questions

EVEN IF YOU KNOW THAT A TEST WILL BE MULTIPLE-CHOICE, YOU STILL DON'T KNOW ALL THAT YOU NEED TO KNOW. There are various types of multiple-choice questions. Some tests will use just one of these kinds. Others will use several, or even all of them. Let's examine the various types of multiple-choice questions you are likely to encounter.

1. The "Who, What, Where Question." This is the simplest, most basic form of multiple-choice question. It asks for you to recall a single, simple fact about the material. For instance:

Where did the Wright Brothers fly their first airplane?

- a. a. Richmond, VA
- b. b. Kitty Hawk, NC
- c. c. Charlotte, NC
- d. d. Philadelphia, PA

The correct answer is B. This question simply asks for you to correctly identify a place name.

2. The "Multiple-Answer" Multiple-choice Question. This one varies from the "Who, What, Where" question in that more than one answer could be correct. It often appears like this:

Which of the following was not a declared war by the U.S. Congress?

I. World War I

II. World War II

III. The Korean War

IV. The Vietnam War

    e. a. I only

    f. b. I and II only

    g. c. III only

    h. d. IV only

    i. e. III and IV only

The correct answer here is E; neither the Korean nor Vietnam Wars were declared a war by Congress. These questions are tricky because many people are tempted, when they see a right answer, to select it, without thinking that there might be another answer that's also right.

3. The "Best Answer" Multiple-choice Question. On this type, the there might not be one clear objective answer, but rather, you're required to select the one that comes closest to being right, or closest to what you believe is right. For example:

The factor which was the most to blame for the 1986 explosion of the Space Shuttle Challenger was:

    j. a. It launched too early in the morning.

    k. b. The cold weather allowed ice to develop.

    l. c. The astronauts did not have enough sleep.

    m. d. The astronauts were not adequately trained.

While it's entirely possible that C or D might have played a role, it's now commonly believed that the cause was the ice which had built up on the Shuttle's "O" rings. Some answers are possible, but B is the best answer.

4. The "Fill in the Blank" Multiple-choice Question. This is frequently used on both grammar and reading comprehension tests. The question is presented as a sentence, with one or two key words left out. You must choose the correct one to fill the blank. Example:

The animals at the zoo _____ by the visitors.

- a. a. Did not feed
- b. b. Cannot fed
- c. c. Should not be fed
- d. d. Never feeding

The answer is C, since "The animals at the zoo should not be fed by the visitors" is the only one which makes good, grammatical sense.

Most the multiple-choice questions you'll encounter will fall into one above category, although it's possible you might also encounter a strange hybrid of two or three types. During your practice for the test, you should practice on each of these four types.

Multiple-Choice Quick Tips

Before looking at specific strategies in detail, lets first look at some general tips that you can use on any test and on multiple-choice questions in any subject. We will explore some of these in more detail later.

- **Finding Hints without Cheating** Pssst. There is a way to get hints about a question, even as you are taking the test—and it is completely legal. The key: Use the test itself to find clues about the answer. Here is how to do this. If you find that a question stumps you, read the answers. If you find one that uses the language that your teacher or textbook used, there is a good chance that this is the right answer. That is because on complex topics, teachers and books tend to always use the same or similar language.

Another point: Look out for test questions which are like previous questions. Often, you will find the same information used in more than one question.

Occasionally you will find the answer to one question contained in another question - be on the lookout for this type of situation and use it to your advantage.

- **Before you try eliminating wrong answers, try to solve the problem.** If you know for sure that you have answered the question correctly, then obviously there is no need to eliminate wrong choices. If you cannot solve it, then see how many choices you can eliminate. Now try solving it again and see if one of the remaining answers comes close to your answer. Your chances of getting the answer right have now improved dramatically. Elimination is one of the most powerful strategies and we will discuss in more detail, as well as practice below.

- **Skip if you do not know.** If you simply do not know the answer and do not know how to get the answer, mark the question in the margin and come back if you have time.

- **Rule out answers that seem so general that they do not offer much information.** If an answer said, for example, "Columbus came to the West in the spring," it is probably not the right answer.

- **Use "all of the above" and "none of the above" to your advantage.** For "all of the above," you need not check to make sure all options are correct. Just check two of them. If two of the answers are correct, then this probably means they are all correct, and you can select "all." (This, of course, is not always the case, especially if there is also an option for "A and B" or "C and D."). Similarly, with "all of the above" questions, you only have to find one wrong answer, and then you have eliminated two choices - one is the wrong answer, and the other is All of the Above.

- **Let "close" answers be your guide.** The clever test-writer often includes an answer that is almost the correct one, to throw you off. The clever test-taker, however, can use this to his advantage. If you see two options that are strangely similar, then chances are good that one of those is the correct choice. That means you can rule out the other answers—and thus improve your chances. For instance, if two choices are George Washington and George Washington Carver, among Abraham Lincoln and Thomas Edison, there is a good chance that one of the two Washingtons is right. More on this strategy below.

Watch Out For Trick Questions

In general, most questions are what they appear to be and over-analyzing is a pitfall to be avoided. However, most multiple-choice tests contain one or two trick questions for a variety of reasons. A trick question is one where the test-writer intentionally makes you think that the answer is easier than it really is. Test-writers include trick questions because so many people think that they have mastered the techniques of taking a test that they need not study the material. In only a very few cases will a test have more than a handful of trick questions. Often instructors will include trick questions, where you really have to know your stuff inside-out to answer it correctly. This separates the "A" students from the "B+" students, and the "A" students from the "A+" students.

The best way to beat the trick question is to read the question carefully and break it down into parts. Then break it down into individual words. For instance, if a question asks,

> "When a plane crashes on the border between the United States and Canada, where are the survivors buried?"

if you had looked at each word individually, you would have realized that the last word, "survivors," means that the test writer is talking about burying people who are still alive.

Before You Change That Answer ...

You are probably familiar with the concept by now: your first instinct is usually right. That is why so many people, when giving advice about tests, tell you that unless you are convinced that your first instinct was wrong, do not take a chance. In those cases, more people change a right answer to the wrong one more often than they change a wrong answer to a right one.

How to Handle This.

Let's take that advice a step further, though. Maybe you do not always have to leave your first answer, especially if you think there might be a reasonable chance that your second choice was right. Before you go changing the answer, though, go on and do a few questions and clear your thoughts of the problem question. After you have done a few more, go back and start over from the beginning. Then see if the original answer is still the one that jumps out at you. If so, leave it. If your second thought now jumps out at you, then go ahead and change it. If both are equal in your mind, then leave it with your first hunch.

Answering Multiple-Choice Step-by-Step

HERE IS A TEST QUESTION:
Which of the following is a helpful tip for taking a multiple-choice test?

e. a. Answering "B" for all questions.

f. b. Eliminate all answers that you know cannot be true.

g. c. Eliminate all answers that seem like they might be true.

h. d. Cheat off your neighbor.

If you answered B, you are correct. Even if you are not positive about the answer, try to get rid of as many options as possible. Think of it this way: If every item on your test has four possible answers, and if you guess on one of those four answers, you have a one-in-four chance (25%) of getting it right. This means you should get one question right for every four that you guess.

However, if you can get rid of two answers, then your chances improve to one-in-two chances, or 50%. That means you will get a correct answer for every two that you guess.

So much for an obvious tip for improving your multiple-choice score. There are many other tips that you may or may not have considered, which will give your grade a boost. Remember, though, that none of these tips are infallible. In fact, some test-writers who know these suggestions deliberately write questions that can confound your system. Usually, however, you will do better on the test if you put these tips into practice.

By familiarizing yourself with these tips, you increase your chances and who knows; you might just get a lucky break and increase your score by a few points!

Answering Step-by-Step.

It might seem complicated and unnecessary to follow a formula for answering a multiple-choice question. After you have practiced this formula for a while, though, it will come naturally and will not take any time at all. Try to follow these steps below on each question.

Step 1. Cover up the answers while you read the question. See the material in your mind's eye and try to envision what the correct answer is before you expose the answers on the answer sheet.

Step 2. Uncover the responses.

Step 3. Eliminate or Estimate. Cross out every choice that you know is ridiculous, absurd or clearly wrong. Then work with the answers that remain.

Step 4. Watch for distracters. A distracter is an answer that looks very similar to the correct answer, but is put there to trip you up. If you see two answers that are strikingly similar, the chances are good that one of them is correct. For instance, if you are asked the term for the distance around a square, and two of the responses are "periwinkle" and "perimeter," you can guess that one of these is probably correct, since the words look similar (both start with "peri-"). Guess one of these two and your chances of correcting selecting "perimeter" are 50/50. More on this below.

Step 5. Check! If you see the answer that you saw in your mind, put a light check-mark by it and then see if any of the other choices are better. If not, mark that response as your answer.

Step 6. If all else fails, guess. If you cannot envision the correct response in your head, or figure it out by reading the passage, and if you are left totally clueless as to what the answer should be, guess.

The MELAB® does NOT penalize for wrong answers - so guessing is a good strategy!

There is a common myth that says choice "C" has a statistically greater chance of being correct. This may be true if your professor is making the test, however, most standardized tests today are generated by computer and the choices are randomized. We do not recommend choosing "C" as a strategy.

That is a quick introduction to multiple-choice to get us warmed up. Next we move onto the strategies and practice test questions section. Each multiple-choice strategy is explained, followed by practice questions using the strategy. Opposite this page is a bubble sheet for answering.

MULTIPLE-CHOICE STRATEGY PRACTICE QUESTIONS ANSWER SHEET.

	A	B	C	D	E		A	B	C	D	E
1	○	○	○	○	○	26	○	○	○	○	○
2	○	○	○	○	○	27	○	○	○	○	○
3	○	○	○	○	○	28	○	○	○	○	○
4	○	○	○	○	○	29	○	○	○	○	○
5	○	○	○	○	○	30	○	○	○	○	○
6	○	○	○	○	○	31	○	○	○	○	○
7	○	○	○	○	○	32	○	○	○	○	○
8	○	○	○	○	○	33	○	○	○	○	○
9	○	○	○	○	○	34	○	○	○	○	○
10	○	○	○	○	○	35	○	○	○	○	○
11	○	○	○	○	○	36	○	○	○	○	○
12	○	○	○	○	○	37	○	○	○	○	○
13	○	○	○	○	○	38	○	○	○	○	○
14	○	○	○	○	○	39	○	○	○	○	○
15	○	○	○	○	○	40	○	○	○	○	○
16	○	○	○	○	○	41	○	○	○	○	○
17	○	○	○	○	○	42	○	○	○	○	○
18	○	○	○	○	○	43	○	○	○	○	○
19	○	○	○	○	○	44	○	○	○	○	○
20	○	○	○	○	○	45	○	○	○	○	○
21	○	○	○	○	○	46	○	○	○	○	○
22	○	○	○	○	○	47	○	○	○	○	○
23	○	○	○	○	○	48	○	○	○	○	○
24	○	○	○	○	○	49	○	○	○	○	○
25	○	○	○	○	○	50	○	○	○	○	○

Multiple-Choice Strategy Practice Questions

THE FOLLOWING ARE DETAILED STRATEGIES FOR ANSWERING MULTIPLE-CHOICE QUESTIONS WITH PRACTICE QUESTIONS FOR EACH STRATEGY.

Answers appear following this section with a detailed explanation and discussion on each strategy and question, plus tips and analysis.

Strategy 1 - Locate Keywords

For every question, figure out exactly what the question is asking by locating key words that are in the question. Underline the keywords to clarify your thoughts and keep on track.

Directions: Read the passage below, and answer the questions using this strategy.

Free-range is a method of farming where animals are allowed to roam freely, instead of being enclosed in a pen. The term is used in two senses that do not overlap completely: as a farmer-centric description of farming methods, and as a consumer-centric description. Farmers practice free-range to achieve free-range or humane certification (and thus capture high prices), to reduce feed costs, to improve the happiness and liveliness of their animals, to produce a higher-quality product, and as a method of raising multiple crops on the same land. [1]

Multiple Choice Strategy

1. The free-range method of farming

    a. Uses a minimum amount of fencing to give animals more room.

    b. Can refer to two different things.

    c. Is always a very humane method.

    d. Only allows for one crop at a time.

2. Free-range farming is practiced

    a. To obtain free-range certification.

    b. To lower the cost of feeding animals.

    c. To produce higher quality product.

    d. All of the above.

3. Free-range farming:

    a. Can mean either farmer described or consumer described methods.

    b. Is becoming much more popular in many areas.

    c. Has many limits and causes prices to go down.

    d. Is only done to make the animals happier and healthier.

4. Free-range certification is most important to farmers because:

    a. Free-range livestock are less expensive to feed.

    b. The price of the product is higher.

    c. Both a and b

    d. The animals are kept in smaller enclosures, so more can be produced.

Strategy 2 - Watch Negatives

For every question, no matter what type, look for negatives. These can include never, not, and others that will completely change what is being asked.

Directions: Read the passage below, and answer the questions using this strategy.

Male grizzly bears can weight more than 1,000 pounds, but typically weigh 400 pounds to 770 pounds. Females are on average 38% smaller, about 250–350 pounds, an example of sexual dimorphism. On average, grizzly bears stand about 1 meter (3.3 ft.) at the shoulder when on all fours, and 2 meters (6.6 ft.) on their hind legs, but males often stand 2.44 meters (8 ft.) or more on their hind legs. On average, grizzly bears from the Yukon River area are about 20% smaller than typical grizzlies. [2]

5. Sexual dimorphism does not mean

    a. Male grizzly bears are the same size as the female of the species.

    b. All grizzly bears look the same and are the same size.

    c. Grizzly bears can be quite large, and weigh more than half a ton.

    d. All of the above

6. The size of a full-grown grizzly bear is never

    a. More than 500 pounds.

    b. Depends on the bear's sex.

    c. Determined simply by diet.

    d. More than 6 feet tall.

7. Grizzly bears from the area of the Yukon River do not

   a. Get as big as most other grizzly bears do

   b. Get the rich and varied food supply needed

   c. Need the same nutrients as other grizzly bears

   d. Get less than 7 feet tall, and weigh close to half of a ton

Strategy 3 - Read the Stem Completely

For every question, no matter what type, read the information in the stem and then try to determine the correct answer before you look at the different answers.

Directions: Read the passage below, and answer the questions using this strategy.

Formerly, taxonomists listed brown and grizzly bears as separate species. Technically, brown and grizzly bears are classified as the same species, Ursus Arctos. The term "brown bear" is commonly used to refer to the members of this species found in coastal areas where salmon is the primary food source. Brown bears found inland and in northern habitats are often called "grizzlies." Brown bears on Kodiak Island are classified as a distinct subspecies from those on the mainland because they are genetically and physically isolated. The shape of their skulls also differs slightly. [3]

8. Grizzly bears, brown bears, and kodiak bears are all

   a. Arctas Ursinas

   b. Ursus Arctos

   c. Arctos Ursina

   d. Ursula Arctic

9. Kodiak brown bears are classified as a different subspecies because

   a. They are much larger than other brown bears

   b. Their diet is radically different from that of other brown bears

   c. They are not true brown bears but instead a mixture of bear species

   d. Of their genetics and head shape, as well as their physical isolation

10. The term grizzlies, when referring to the brown bear, is used mainly

   a. In eastern areas where the bear grows large

   b. Only in snowy areas where there are low year round temperatures

   c. In the northern and inland areas

   d. In areas where the bear has a silver appearance

11. The term brown bear is normally used

   a. When one of the main food sources is salmon

   b. When the bear is small

   c. When the bear is found inland

   d. When the bear has a light brown coat and is very large

Strategy 4 - Consider all the Choices Before Deciding

For every question, no matter what type, make sure to read every option before making your choice.

Directions: Read the passage below, and answer the questions using this strategy.

Jim Martell, a hunter from Idaho, reportedly found and shot a grizzly-polar bear hybrid near Sachs Harbor on Banks Island, Northwest Territories, Canada, on April 16, 2006. Martell had been hunting for polar bears with an official license and a guide, at a cost of $50,000, and killed the animal believing it to be a normal polar bear. Officials took interest in the creature after noticing that it had thick, creamy white fur, typical of polar bears, as well as long claws; a humped back; a shallow face; and brown patches around its eyes, nose, and back, as well as patches on one foot, which are all traits of grizzly bears. If the bear had been adjudicated to be a grizzly, he would have faced a possible CAN$1,000 fine and up to a year in jail. A DNA test conducted by the Wildlife Genetics International in British Columbia confirmed that it was a hybrid, with the mother a polar bear and the father a grizzly. It is the first documented case in the wild, though it was known that this hybrid was biologically possible and other hybrids have been bred in zoos in the past. [4]

12. Which grizzly bear features did the hybrid bear have?

    a. Brown patches in certain areas

    b. Long claws

    c. A shallow face

    d. All of the above

13. The hybrid bear was the result of

    a. A male brown bear and a female grizzly.

    b. A female brown bear and a male grizzly bear.

    c. A female polar bear and a male grizzly bear.

    d. A male polar bear and a female grizzly.

14. The hybrid bear tested in this case was

    a. The first case ever known where two different bear species mated successfully.

    b. Genetically flawed and prone to many diseases and conditions.

    c. A fluke, and a mistake of nature which has never happened.

    d. The first proof of a wild bear hybrid species outside of zoos.

15. Modern science

   a. Has proven that the cubs from two different species will not survive in almost every case.

   b. Has known for some time that these hybrid bears were possible.

   c. Completely understands how bear hybrids occur and why this happens in nature.

   d. Has studied hundreds of bear hybrids in an attempt to learn more.

Strategy 5 - Elimination

For every question, no matter what type, eliminating obviously incorrect answers narrows the possible choices. Elimination is probably the most powerful strategy for answering multiple-choice.

Directions: Read the passage below, and answer the questions using this strategy.

The male peafowl, or peacock, has long been known and valued for its brilliant tail feathers. The bright spots on it are known as "eyes," and inspired the Greek myth that Hera placed the hundred eyes of the slain giant Argus on the tail of her favorite bird. Indian Peafowl are iridescent blue-green or blue in the head, neck and breast.

The back, or scapular, feathers are vermiculated in black and white, while the primaries are orange-chestnut. The so-called "tail" of the peacock, also termed the "train," is not the tail quill feathers but highly elongated upper tail feathers. It is mostly bronze-green, with a series of eyes that are best seen when the train is fanned. The actual tail feathers are short and grey-colored and can be seen from behind when a peacock's train is fanned in a courtship display.

During the molting season, the males shed their stunning train feathers and reveal the unassuming grey-colored tail, which is normally hidden from view beneath the train. The female peacock is duller in comparison. It is mostly brown, with pale under-parts and some green iridescence in the neck, and lacks the long upper tail feathers of the male. [5]

16. The long colorful tail feathers of the peacock

    a. Are only present in the male of the species

    b. Are used by both sexes to warn off predators

    c. Are normally red and blue in color

    d. Are only present for a very short time each year

17. The differences between the male and female peacock are

    a. Size and weight

    b. Coloring and tail feather length

    c. The female does not ever leave the nest

    d. The male sits on and hatches the eggs

18. The term peacock actually refers to

    a. Both sexes from the pheasant family

    b. The eyes on the tail feathers of the bird

    c. The male bird of the peafowl species

    d. The female bird of the peafowl species

19. The gray tail feathers on the male peacock can be seen

    a. When the bird is startled

    b. Only when the bird is searching for food

    c. When the peacock lowers the tail feathers to the ground

    d. During molting

Strategy 6 - Opposites

For every question, no matter what type, look at answers that are opposites. When two answers are opposites, the odds increase that one of them is the correct answer.

Directions: Read the passage below, and answer the questions using this strategy.

Smallpox is an infectious disease unique to humans, caused by either of two virus variants, the Variola Major or Variola Minor. The disease is also known by the Latin names Variola or Variola vera, which is a derivative of the Latin varius, meaning spotted.

Smallpox localizes in small blood vessels of the skin and in the mouth and throat. In the skin, this results in a characteristic rash, and later, blisters. Variola Major produces a more serious disease and has an overall mortality rate of 30–35%. Variola Minor causes a milder form of disease (also known as alastrim, cottonpox, milkpox, whitepox, and Cuban itch) which kills about 1% of its victims. Long-term complications of Variola major infection include characteristic scars, commonly on the face, which occur in 65–85% of survivors. Blindness and limb deformities due to arthritis and osteomyelitis are less common complications, seen in about 2–5% of cases.
6

20. Smallpox

    a. Effects all mammals, including humans

    b. Is caused by a bacteria from contact with dead flesh

    c. Was called the great pox during the fifteenth century

    d. Only affects humans, although other species can carry and transmit the virus

21. Smallpox caused by Variola major has a

    a. Thirty to thirty five percent survival rate

    b. Sixty percent mortality rate

    c. Thirty to thirty five percent mortality rate

    d. Sixty percent survival rate

22. Smallpox caused by Variola minor is

a. Much more severe, with a greater number of pox and more scarring

b. Much less severe, with fewer pox and less scarring

c. Characterized because there are no pox

d. So minor that no treatment or medical attention is needed

23. Smallpox can be fatal

a. In between thirty and thirty five percent of those who catch the virus, depending on the type

b. In between thirty and sixty five percent of those who catch the virus, depending on the type

c. When no medical treatment is available

d. Only in developing countries where medical care is poor

Strategy 7 - Look for Differences

For every question, no matter what type, look at the two choices that seem to be correct and then examine the differences between the two. Refer to the stem to determine the best answer.

Directions: Read the passage below, and answer the questions using this strategy.

Lightning is an atmospheric discharge of electricity accompanied by thunder, which typically occurs during thunderstorms, and sometimes during volcanic eruptions or dust storms. Atmospheric electrical discharges, or bolts of lightning, can travel at speeds of 130,000 mph, and reach temperatures approaching 54,000° F. This is hot enough to fuse silica sand into glass channels, known as fulgurites, that are normally hollow and can extend some distance into the ground. There are some 16 million lightning storms in the world every year.

The irrational fear of lightning and thunder is astraphobia.

Lightning can also occur within the ash clouds of volcanic

eruptions, or can be caused by violent forest fires which generate sufficient dust to create a static charge.

How lightning initially forms is still a matter of debate: Scientists have studied root causes ranging from atmospheric perturbations (wind, humidity, friction, and atmospheric pressure) to the impact of solar wind and accumulation of charged solar particles. Ice inside a cloud is thought to be a key element in lightning development, and may cause a forcible separation of positive and negative charges within the cloud, thus helping in the formation of lightning. [z]

24. Astraphobia is

    a. Fear of thunder

    b. Fear of thunder and lightning

    c. Fear of lightning

    d. None of the above

25. Lightning occurs

    a. Only in thunderstorms

    b. In thunderstorms and dust storms

    c. In thunderstorms, volcanic eruptions and dust storms

    d. In the upper atmosphere

26. Fulgurites are

    a. Made of silica

    b. Made of glass

    c. Made of silica turned in to glass

    d. Made of silica and glass

Strategy 8 - Context clues

Looked at the sentences and the context to determine the best option. Sometimes, the answer may be located right in the passage or question.

Directions: Read the passage below, and answer the questions using this strategy.

Venus is one of the four solar terrestrial planets, meaning that, like the Earth, it is a rocky body. In size and mass, it is very similar to the Earth, and is often described as its "sister," or Earth's twin. The diameter of Venus is only 650 km. less than the Earth's, and its mass is 81.5% of the Earth's. However, conditions on the Venusian surface differ radically from those on Earth, due to its dense carbon dioxide atmosphere. The mass of the atmosphere of Venus is 96.5% carbon dioxide, with most of the remaining 3.5% nitrogen.

Venus is the second-closest planet to the Sun, orbiting every 224.7 Earth days. The planet is named after Venus, the Roman goddess of love and beauty. After the Moon, it is the brightest natural object in the night sky, reaching an apparent magnitude of −4.6. Because Venus is an inferior planet from Earth, it never appears to venture far from the Sun: its elongation reaches a maximum of 47.8°. Venus reaches its maximum brightness shortly before sunrise or shortly after sunset, and is often called the Morning Star or the Evening Star. [8]

27. Apparent magnitude is

    a. A measure of darkness

    b. A measure of brightness

    c. The distance from the moon

    d. The distance from the earth

28. The elongation of a planet is

   a. The angular distance from the sun, as seen from earth.

   b. The distance from the sun

   c. The distance form the earth

   d. None of the above

29. Terrestrial planets are

   a. Made of rock

   b. Have people on them

   c. The earth and no others

   d. The same size as Earth

30. How many planets orbit the sun in less than 224.7 days?

   a. 1 planet

   b. Only Venus

   c. 2 planets

   d. 3 planets

Strategy 9 - Try Every Option

For definition questions, try out all the options - one option will fit better than the rest. As you go through the options, use Strategy 5 - Elimination, to eliminate obviously incorrect choices as you go.

Directions: Read the passage below, and answer the questions using this strategy.

On Earth, common weather phenomena include wind, cloud, rain, snow, fog and dust storms. Less common events include natural disasters such as tornadoes, hurricanes, typhoons and ice storms. Almost all weather phenomena occurs in the troposphere (the lower part of the atmosphere). Weather does occur in the stratosphere and can affect weather lower down in the troposphere, but the exact mechanisms are poorly understood.

Weather occurs primarily due to different temperature and moisture densities. The strong temperature contrast between polar and tropical air gives rise to the jet stream. Weather systems in the mid-latitudes, such as extra-tropical cyclones, are caused by instabilities of the jet stream flow. Weather systems in the tropics, such as monsoons or thunderstorms, are caused by different processes.

Because the Earth's axis is tilted relative to its orbital plane, sunlight is incident at different angles at different times of the year. In June the Northern Hemisphere is tilted towards the sun, so at any given Northern Hemisphere latitude, sunlight is more direct than in December. This effect causes seasons. Over thousands to hundreds of thousands of years, changes in Earth's orbital parameters affect the amount and distribution of solar energy received by the Earth and influence long-term climate. [9]

31. The troposphere is

    a. The highest strata of the atmosphere

    b. The lowest strata of the atmosphere

    c. The middle level of the atmosphere

    d. Not part of the atmosphere

32. Monsoons are

    a. Caused by instabilities in the jet stream

    b. Caused by processes other than instabilities in the jet stream

    c. Part of the jet stream

    d. Cause the jet stream

33. Extra-tropical cyclones occur

   a. In the tropics

   b. In temperate zones

   c. In the gulf stream

   d. In mid-latitudes

34. Tilted means:

   a. Slanted

   b. Rotating

   c. Connected to

   d. Bent

Strategy 10 - Work for it

For questions about supporting details, work is the key. Review the passage to locate the right option. Never forget the choices that you are given are designed to confuse, and they may *seem* reasonable answers. However, if they are not mentioned in the text, they are "red herring" answers.

The best answer is the exact answer mentioned in the text.

Directions: Read the passage below, and answer the questions using this strategy.

Ebola is the common term for a group of viruses belonging to genus Ebola virus (EBOV), which is a part of the family Filoviridae, and for the disease that they cause, Ebola hemorrhagic fever. The virus is named after the Ebola River, where the first recognized outbreak of Ebola hemorrhagic fever occurred.

The viruses are characterized by long filaments, and have a shape similar to that of the Marburg virus, also in the family Filoviridae, and possessing similar disease symptoms. There are several species within the Ebola virus genus, which in turn have several specific strains or serotypes.

The Zaire virus is the type species, which is also the first discovered and the most lethal. Ebola is transmitted primarily through bodily fluids, and to a limited extent through skin. The virus interferes with the endothelial cells lining the interior surface of blood vessels and platelet cells. As the blood vessel walls become damaged and the platelets are unable to coagulate, patients succumb to hypovolemic shock.

Ebola first emerged in 1976 in Zaire. It remained largely obscure until 1989 with the outbreak in Reston, Virginia.[10]

35. The Ebola virus received this name because of

    a. The doctor who first discovered the virus

    b. The cure that is used to treat those infected

    c. The river where the disease was first encountered

    d. What the virus does to the body

36. Viruses in the Ebola genus are recognizable

    a. Because of their hooked shape

    b. Because of their long filaments

    c. Due to their oblong heads

    d. Because of their unique color

37. One of the most common causes of death from the Ebola family of viruses is

    a. Hypovolemic shock due to blood vessel damage

    b. Bleeding of the brain that cannot be stopped

    c. A heart attack from blood loss and lack of fluids

    d. A high fever that cannot be lowered

38. The most deadly strain of the Ebola virus family is the

    a. The Reston strain

    b. The Ivory Coast strain

    c. The Zaire strain

    d. The Sudan strain

Strategy 11 - Look at the Big Picture

Details can be tricky when dealing with main idea and summary questions, but do not let the details distract you. Look at the big picture instead of the smaller parts to determine the right answer.

Directions: Read the passage below, and answer the questions using this strategy.

As of late 2005, three fruit bat species have been identified as carrying the Ebola virus but not showing disease symptoms. They are now believed to be a natural host species, or reservoir, of the virus. Plants, arthropods, and birds have also been considered as reservoirs; however, bats are considered the most likely candidate.

Bats were known to reside in the cotton factory where the first outbreaks in 1976 and 1979 occurred, and they have also been implicated in Marburg infections in 1975 and 1980. Of 24 plant species and 19 vertebrate species experimentally inoculated with Ebola virus, only bats became infected. The absence of clinical signs in these bats is characteristic of a reservoir species.

In 2002-03, a survey of 1,030 animals from Gabon and the Republic of the Congo including 679 bats found Ebola virus RNA in 13 fruit bats (Hypsignathus monstrosus, Epomops franquetti and Myonycteris torquata). Bats are also known to be the reservoirs for several related viruses including Nipah virus, Hendra virus and Lyssa viruses.[11]

39. The species most suspected as a potential Ebola virus reservoir is

    a. Birds
    b. Insects
    c. Plants
    d. Bats

40. Most plant and animal species

   a. Can carry the Ebola virus but not become infected

   b. Can not carry and transmit the Ebola virus

   c. Are responsible for new cases of Ebola viruses

   d. Can be infected with one of the Ebola viruses

41. Bats are known for

   a. Being carriers of many different viruses, including Ebola

   b. Transmitting the Ebola virus through a scratch

   c. Being susceptible to the virus and becoming infected

   d. Transmitting the Ebola virus through infected droppings

Strategy 12 - Best Possible Answer

Try to determine the best possible answer according to the information given in the passage. Do not be distracted by answers that seem correct or are mostly correct.

Directions: Read the passage below, and answer the questions using this strategy.

In the early stages, Ebola may not be highly contagious. Contact with someone in early stages may not even transmit the disease. As the illness progresses, bodily fluids represent an extreme biohazard.

Due to lack of proper equipment and hygienic practices, large-scale epidemics occur mostly in poor, isolated areas without modern hospitals or well-educated medical staff. Many areas where the infectious reservoir exists have just these characteristics.

In such environments, all that can be done is immediately cease all needle sharing or use without adequate sterilization procedures, to isolate patients, and to observe strict barrier nursing procedures with the use of a medical-rated disposable face mask, gloves, goggles, and a gown always. This should be strictly enforced for all medical personnel and visitors. [12]

42. Ebola is highly contagious

    a. Only when blood is present

    b. Only in the first stages before hemorrhaging occurs

    c. At all stages of the illness from incubation to recovery

    d. Only in the later stages when the virus is very numerous

43. Exposure to the Ebola virus means

    a. A death sentence for most patients

    b. Isolation for the patient, and proper precautions for all medical personnel to contain the virus

    c. The virus will spread rapidly and there is no treatment available

    d. A full recovery usually, with very few symptoms

44. Ebola outbreaks commonly occur

    a. Because sterilization and containment procedures are not followed or available

    b. Due to infected animals in the area

    c. Because of rat droppings in homes

    d. Because of a contaminated water supply

45. Ebola is

    a. More common in advanced nations where treatment makes the disease minor

    b. More common in third world and developing countries

    c. Fatal in more than ninety-five percent of the cases

    d. Highly contagious during the incubation period

Answers to Sample Multiple-Choice Strategy Questions

Strategy 1 - Keywords in the question tells what the question is asking

1. B

The question asks about the free range *method* of farming. Here method refers to *type* of farming. "Method" here is the keyword and can be marked or underlined.

2. D

The Question is, "Free-range farming is *practiced* ..." The keyword here is "practiced." Looking at the choices, which all start with "to," it is clear the answer will be about *why* free range ... Also notice that one choice is "All of the above," which here, is the correct answer. However, when "All of the above" is an option, this is a potential Elimination strategy. All you have to do is find one option that is incorrect and you can use Strategy 5 - Elimination to eliminate two choices and increase your odds from one in four, to one in two.

3. A

The question is, "Free range farming husbandry ..." From the question, and the *lack* of keywords, together with the choices presented, the answer will be a definition free range farming husbandry.

4. C

The question is, "Free-range certification is *most important* to farmers because ... " The keywords here are "most important." Be careful to choose the best possible answer.

Strategy 2 - Negatives.

These four questions all have negatives: does not mean, is never, do not, and is not. These questions exclude possibilities, so if you see any choices that are true, you can eliminate them right away.

5. D

The question asks what sexual dimorphism does *not* mean. Circle the word "not" and keep it firmly in mind. Next, what is sexual dimorphism. Reading the text quickly, sexual dimorphism is not defined explicitly, but related to the female bears being smaller than the males. Probably there are other aspects, but this general definition is all that is needed to answer the question.

First, notice that "All of the above" is choice D. In addition the question is a negative. So in order for choice D to be correct, choices A, B and C must be *in*correct. This narrows down your options. If any of choices A, B or C are correct, then you can eliminate that choice as well as choice D.

Either all the choices are *in*correct, in which case, choice D, "All of the above" is correct.

Choice A, male and females are the same size is incorrect. Choice B, all grizzly bears look the same and are the same size, is incorrect. Choice C, grizzly bears (plural so *all* grizzly bears) can be large and weigh more than half a ton. This is incorrect since while all grizzly bears are large, female bears weight less than half a ton.

All three choices are incorrect so choice D is the correct answer, "All of the Above," are incorrect.

6. A

First, circle or underline never to show this is a negative question. Now look at the options to find an option that is not true.

Choice A is true as male bears are 1,000 pounds. Place a mark beside this one. It may be tempting to select this option as your answer, but it is important to look at all choices before making a final decision.

Choice B is not true - size does not depend on the sex.
Choice C is not true - size does not depend on diet.
Choice D is not true - males often stand 8 feet.

So choice A is correct.

7. A
First circle "do not" to mark this as a negative question.

Choice A is correct, Yukon River grizzly bears do not get as big as other grizzlies, so put a mark beside it for later consideration. Examine the other choices before making a final decision.

Choice B is not mentioned in the text, and can be eliminated.

Choice C is not mentioned in the text and can be eliminated.

Choice D is true, but this is a negative question so it is false.

Some of the above choices may be true from a common sense point of view, but if they aren't mentioned specifically in the passage, they can be eliminated.

Choice A is correct.

Strategy 3 - Read the stem completely.

Read the question, and then look for the answer in the text before reading the choices. Reading the choices first will confuse, just as it is meant to do! Do not fall into this trap!

8. B
The choices here are very confusing and are meant to be! Four variations on the latin species name, Ursus Arctos are given, so the question is what version of this latin name is correct, which gives a very straight-forward strategy to solving. Since the name is latin, it is going to stand out in the text. Take the first option, "Arctas Ursinas," and scan the text for something that looks like that. At the end of the second sentence is "Ursus Arctos," which is very close. Next confirm what this sentence refers to, which gives the correct answer, choice B.

9. D
This question asks why Kodiak brown bears are a different subspecies, and the options are designed to confuse a careless, stressed test-taker. Scan the text for "Kodiak," which appears in the second to last sentence, and answers the question.

10. C
This question asks about the relationship between brown bears and grizzly bears. If you are not careful you will be confused by the choices.

11. A
Read the question, then read the text before trying to answer and avoid confusion.

Strategy 4 - Consider all choices before deciding.

In Strategy 3, we learned to find the correct answer in the text before reading the choices. OK, now you have read the text and have the right answer. The next thing is Strategy 4 - Read *all* the choices. Once you have read all the choices, select the correct choice.

12. D
First, notice that "All of the above" is a choice. So if you find one option that is incorrect, you can eliminate that option and option D, "All of the above." Reading the question first, (Strategy #3) then looking in the text, and then reading all the choices before answering, you can see that choices A, B and C are all correct, so choice D, All of the Above, is the correct choice.
If you had not read all the choices first, then you might be tempted to impulsively choose A, B, or C.

13. C
Looking at the choices, they are designed to confuse with different choices and combinations. Recognizing this, it is therefore important to be extra careful in making your choice. If you are stressed, in a hurry, or not paying attention, you will probably get this question wrong by making an impulsive choice and not reading through all the choices before making a selection.

Referring to the text, you will find the sentence, "... it was a hybrid, with the mother a polar bear and the father a grizzly," which answers the question.

14. D
Reading through all the choices, B and C can be eliminated

right away as they are not referred to in the text. They might appear as good answers but they are not from the passage.

Looking at choices A and D, the issue is if this has happened before, or has it happened only in zoos. Referring to the text, the last sentence tells us the answer, "It is the first documented case in the wild, though it was known that this hybrid was biologically possible and other hybrids have been bred in zoos in the past."

15. B
Reading through the four choices, the question concerns, what does science know? Does it happen all the time? Completely understood? They do survive? Is it possible? Look in the text for how much is known. The last sentence, "It is the first documented case in the wild, though it was known that this hybrid was biologically possible" gives the answer.

Strategy 5 - Elimination.

For every question, no matter what type, eliminating obviously incorrect answers narrows the possible choices. Elimination is probably the most powerful strategy for answering multiple-choice.

16. A
Using this strategy the choices can be narrowed down to choices A and D. I have never seen a peacock with red in their tail, so choice C can *probably* be eliminated, but check back. Most birds and many animals have a pattern where the male is colorful and the female less colorful. Choice B can be eliminated as it refers to "both sexes" having colorful tails. Choice D is a good candidate as the text refers to molting season, however, the text does not say how long this is, so there is some doubt. This makes choice A the best choice as it is referred to directly in the text.

17. B
Choice D can be eliminated right away, as it is rare for a male bird to sit on eggs.

Skimming the passage, choices A and C can be eliminated, as they are not mentioned directly in the text, leaving only choice D.

18. C
Choices A and D can be eliminated right away, since "cock" always refers to a male bird. Referring to the text, "The male peafowl, or peacock, has long been …" making choice C the best choice.

19. D
Choices A and B can be eliminated either right away or with a quick check of the passage, since they are not mentioned. Choice C is suspicious since the grey feathers are under the tail feathers, so it is difficult to see how they could be visible when the tail feathers are lowered.

Strategy 6 - Opposites

If there are opposites, one of them is generally the correct answer. If it helps, make a table that lays out the different options and the correct option will become clear.

20. D
Notice that choices A and D are opposites. Referring to the text, "Smallpox is an infectious disease unique to humans …" eliminates choice A. Also notice choices B and C are not mentioned in the text and can be eliminated right away.

21. C
Notice that all the choices are opposites. 30 - 35% mortality, or survival rate, or 60%. Therefore, the task is to review the text, looking for 30% or 60%, survival or mortality, stay clear, and do not get confused. Sometimes making notes or a table can help to clarify.

The question is asking about percent, so it is easy and fast to skim the passage for a percent sign.

The first percent sign is in the second paragraph, 30 - 35%. Write this in the margin. Next, see what this percent refers to, which is the mortality rate. Write "mortality" next to 30 - 35%. Now, working backwards, see what the 30 - 35% mortality rate refers to. At the beginning of that sentence, is Variola Major.

30 - 35%	Mortality	V. Major

Now we have a clear understanding of what the passage is saying, which we have retrieved quickly and easily, and now hopefully we will not get confused by the different choices.

Choices A and B can be eliminated right away. Choice C looks correct. Check choice D quickly, and confirm that it is incorrect. Choice C is the correct answer.

22. B
Choices A and B are opposites. Is Variola Minor more or less severe, with more or fewer pox, and more or less scarring? The other two choices, "no pox" and "no treatment" can be eliminated quickly. Either choice A or B are going to be wrong.

Make a quick table like this:

Major - more serious - scars, blindness
Minor - milder

The passage does not mention scarring from Variola minor, but we can infer that it is milder. Looking at the options, choice A is clearly talking about Variola major, and we can infer that choice B is talking about Variola minor and is the correct answer. We can confirm our inference from the text.

Also note the words, 'major' and 'minor.' Which gives a clue concerning severity, and the elimination of choice A.

23. A
Choices A and B are not exactly opposite, but very close and designed to confuse if you do not read them properly. How many people die from the virus? Between 30 and 35%? Or between 35 and 60%? Scan the text with these numbers in mind.

This question is asking about a percent figures, so quickly scan the passage for a percent sign, which first appears in the second paragraph. Working back, confirm that the percent figures is related to mortality, which it is.

Strategy 7 - Look for Differences.

Look at two choices that appear to be correct and examine them carefully.

24. B
Choices A, B and C are very similar and designed to confuse and distract someone who does not look carefully at the text. What is astraphobia exactly? This is a definition question for an unusual word, astraphobia. Scan the text for "astraphobia." Choice B is correct.

25. C
Choices A, B and C are similar and designed to confuse, or tempt a stressed or careless test-taker into making a quick and incorrect choice. Checking the passage, in the first paragraph, lightning occurs in thunderstorms, volcanic eruptions and in dust storms, so choice C is correct.

26. C
All four answers are similar and designed to confuse. Seeing how similar the choices are, it is very important to be clear on the exact definition. Scan the text quickly for the word "fulgurites." From the first paragraph, fulgurites are formed when lightning is "... hot enough to fuse silica sand into glass channels ..." so the correct answer, and the option that answers the question best, is choice C, "Made of silica turned into glass."

Strategy 8 - Context clues.

Look at the sentences and the context to determine the best option. Sometimes, the answer may be located right in the passage or question.

27. B
You do not have to know the exact meaning - just enough to answer the question. The phrase is used in the passage, "After the Moon, it is the brightest natural object in the night sky, reaching an apparent magnitude of −4.6" where Venus is compared to the brightness of the moon, so the apparent magnitude must have something to do with brightness, which is enough information to answer the question. Notice also, how the choices are opposites. Choice A and B are op-

posites as are choices C and D.

28. A
The exact meaning is not necessary, you only need only enough information to answer the question. The passage where this phrase is used is, "Because Venus is an inferior planet from Earth, it never appears to venture far from the Sun: its elongation reaches a maximum of 47.8°." Elongation in this sentence is something connected with distance from the sun, but also something to do with Earth. Choice C can be eliminated right away, and since one choice is wrong, Choice D, All of the Above, can also be eliminated. Choice A is the most likely correct because it mentions, "as seen from earth."

29. A
Choices C and D can be eliminated right away. No mention is made of size or people, so choices C and D are also incorrect. Terrestrial has many similar meanings, but choice A is the best. From the passage, "Venus is one of the four solar terrestrial planets, meaning that, like the Earth, it is a rocky body."

Note that choice B is a grammatical error and can be eliminated right away. The question is, "Terrestrial planets are," and choice B is, "Have people on them."

This is a great strategy, looking for grammatical errors and eliminating, and what you might expect to see on a test that a professor has made themselves. However, most standardized tests are generated by computer, and proofed by many different people who have considerable expertise in correcting this type of easy question. Keep this in mind because it is an easy elimination, but don't expect to see this type of thing on a standardized test.

30. A
This is a bit of a trick question and designed to confuse, as it requires an additional step of logical reasoning. Referring to the text, Venus is the *second* closest planet to the sun so there must be one planet that is closer. Planets closer to the sun will rotate the sun faster, so the answer must be choice A.

Strategy 9 - Try out every option for word meaning questions.

For definition questions, try out all the options - one option will fit better than the rest. As you go through the options, use Strategy 5 - Elimination, to eliminate obviously incorrect choices as you go.

31. B
The answer is taken directly from the passage. Notice that choices A and B are opposites, so one of them will be incorrect. Look in the text carefully for the exact definition. If you are uncertain, make a table in the margin.

Scan the passage looking for the word you are asked to define. Large or unusual words generally stand out and can be located quickly. Once you have found the position in the passage of the word using quick reading scanning techniques, then focus on the sentence and read carefully.

32. B
The sentences talking about the jet stream and monsoons are next to one another. Trying each definition, and comparing to the text, only choice B fits. If you are uncertain, copy the information from the passage into a table.

The question is, what is the relationship between monsoons and the jet stream.

Scan the passage for "jet stream" and "monsoon."

Tropical cyclones	Jet stream
Monsoons and thunderstorms	Different processes

33. D
Referring to the passage, and trying each definition choice, choice D is the only answer that makes sense referring to the text.

34. A
The passage from the text is, "Because the Earth's axis is tilted relative to its orbital plane, sunlight is incident at different angles at different times of the year." Substituting all

the choices given into this sentence, slanted, choice A, is the only sensible answer. Here is what substitutions look like:

> a. In June the Northern Hemisphere is *slanted* towards the sun...
>
> b. In June the Northern Hemisphere is *rotating* towards the sun...
>
> c. In June the Northern Hemisphere is *connected to* towards the sun...
>
> d. In June the Northern Hemisphere is *bent* towards the sun...

Choice A is the only one that makes sense.

Strategy 10 - You have to work for it! Check carefully for supporting details.

All answers can be found by carefully reading the text. The questions paraphrase the text found in the passage.

35. C
The passage has a lot of details so read carefully and stay clear.

36. B
The choices are designed to confuse. Check the text for the exact definition and do not be distracted by other choices.

37. A
Here is a quick tip. On choice A, the word hypovolemic is used. This is an unusual word and specific medical vocabulary. None of the other choices uses any specific vocabulary like this, so it is very likely to be the right answer. You can quickly scan the text for this word to confirm. Scanning the text for an unusual word is easy and fast, and one of the most powerful techniques for this type of question.

38. C
Scan the text for Zaire.

Strategy 11 - Look at the big picture

Details can be tricky when dealing with main idea and summary questions, but do not let the details distract you. Look at the big picture instead of the smaller parts to determine the right answer.

39. D
The passage says in 2005 it was found there are 3 fruit bat species most suspected of carrying the virus. The details (3 species, fruit bats and 2005) do not matter. Only the fact that bats are suspected.

40. B
The relevant passage is, "Of 24 plant species and 19 vertebrate species experimentally inoculated with Ebola virus, only bats became infected." The inference is that these plant and animal species cannot be infected, (i.e. carry and transmit the disease) so choice B is correct.

41. A
The relevant passage is, "Bats are also known to be the reservoirs for several related viruses including Nipah virus, Hendra virus and Lyssaviruses."

Strategy 12 - Make the best choice based on the information given.

42. D
Choices B and C are incorrect by the passage, "In the early stages, Ebola may not be highly contagious." Choice A is not mentioned, leaving choice D.

43. B
The passage does not say anything about the information in choices A and D. Choice C is irrelevant to the question.

44. A
Choices B and C are not mentioned in the passage. Choice D is a good possibility, however, choice A covers choice D and is referred to in the passage.

45. B
Choice A is incorrect. Choices C and D are not mentioned.

Practice Questions Answer Sheet

	A	B	C	D	E		A	B	C	D	E
1	○	○	○	○	○	21	○	○	○	○	○
2	○	○	○	○	○	22	○	○	○	○	○
3	○	○	○	○	○	23	○	○	○	○	○
4	○	○	○	○	○	24	○	○	○	○	○
5	○	○	○	○	○	25	○	○	○	○	○
6	○	○	○	○	○						
7	○	○	○	○	○						
8	○	○	○	○	○						
9	○	○	○	○	○						
10	○	○	○	○	○						
11	○	○	○	○	○						
12	○	○	○	○	○						
13	○	○	○	○	○						
14	○	○	○	○	○						
15	○	○	○	○	○						
16	○	○	○	○	○						
17	○	○	○	○	○						
18	○	○	○	○	○						
19	○	○	○	○	○						
20	○	○	○	○	○						

Reading Comprehension Practice Questions

Questions 1 - 4 refer to the following passage.

Passage 1: "If You Have Allergies, You're Not Alone"

People who experience allergies might joke that their immune systems have let them down or are seriously lacking. Truthfully though, people who experience allergic reactions or allergy symptoms during certain times of the year have heightened immune systems that are, "better" than those of people who have perfectly healthy but less militant immune systems.

Still, when a person has an allergic reaction, they are having an adverse reaction to a substance that is considered normal to most people. Mild allergic reactions usually have symptoms like itching, runny nose, red eyes, or bumps or discoloration of the skin. More serious allergic reactions, such as those to animal and insect poisons or certain foods, may result in the closing of the throat, swelling of the eyes, low blood pressure, an inability to breathe, and can even be fatal.

Different treatments help different allergies, and which one a person uses depends on the nature and severity of the allergy. It is recommended to patients with severe allergies to take extra precautions, such as carrying an EpiPen, which treats anaphylactic shock and may prevent death, always in order for the remedy to be readily available and more effective. When an allergy is not so severe, treatments may be used just relieve a person of uncomfortable symptoms. Over the counter allergy medicines treat milder symptoms, and can be bought at any grocery store and used in moderation to help people with allergies live normally.

There are many tests available to assess whether a person has allergies or what they may be allergic to, and advances in these tests and the medicine used to treat patients continues to improve. Despite this fact, allergies still affect many people throughout the year or even every day. Medicines used to treat allergies have side effects of their own, and it is difficult to bring the body into balance with the use of medicine. Regardless, many of those who live with allergies are grateful for what is available and find it useful in maintaining their lifestyles.

1. According to this passage, it can be understood that the word "militant" belongs in a group with the words:

    a. sickly, ailing, faint

    b. strength, power, vigor

    c. active, fighting, warring

    d. worn, tired, breaking down

2. The author says that "medicines used to treat allergies have side effects of their own" to

    a. point out that doctors aren't very good at diagnosing and treating allergies

    b. argue that because of the large number of people with allergies, a cure will never be found

    c. explain that allergy medicines aren't cures and some compromise must be made

    d. argue that more wholesome remedies should be researched and medicines banned

3. It can be inferred that _____ recommend that some people with allergies carry medicine with them.

    a. the author

    b. doctors

    c. the makers of EpiPen

    d. people with allergies

4. The author has written this passage to

    a. inform readers on symptoms of allergies so people with allergies can get help

    b. persuade readers to be proud of having allergies

    c. inform readers on different remedies so people with allergies receive the right help

    d. describe different types of allergies, their symptoms, and their remedies

Questions 5 - 8 refer to the following passage.

Passage 2: "When a Poet Longs to Mourn, He Writes an Elegy"

Poems are an expressive, especially emotional, form of writing. They have been present in literature virtually from the time civilizations invented the written word. Poets often portrayed as moody, secluded, and even troubled, but this is because poets are introspective and feel deeply about the current events and cultural norms they are surrounded with. Poets often produce the most telling literature, giving insight into the society and mind-set they come from. This can be done in many forms.

The oldest types of poems often include many stanzas, may or may not rhyme, and are more about telling a story than experimenting with language or words. The most common types of ancient poetry are epics, which are usually extremely long stories that follow a hero through his journey, or elegies, which are often solemn in tone and used to mourn or lament something or someone. The Mesopotamians are often said to have invented the written word, and their literature is among the oldest in the world, including the epic poem titled "Epic of Gilgamesh." Similar in style and length to "Gilgamesh" is "Beowulf," an elegy poem written in Old English and set in Scandinavia. These poems are often used by professors as the earliest examples of literature.

The importance of poetry was revived in the Renaissance.

At this time, Europeans discovered the style and beauty of ancient Greek arts, and poetry was among those. Shakespeare is the most well-known poet of the time, and he used poetry not only to write poems but also to write plays for the theater. The most popular forms of poetry during the Renaissance included villanelles (a nineteen-line poem with two rhymes throughout), sonnets, as well as the epic. Poets during this time focused on style and form, and developed very specific rules and outlines for how an exceptional poem should be written.

As often happens in the arts, modern poets have rejected the constricting rules of Renaissance poets, and free form poems are much more popular. Some modern poems would read just like stories if they weren't arranged into lines and stanzas. It is difficult to tell which poems and poets will be the most important, because works of art often become more famous in hindsight, after the poet has died and society can look at itself without being in the moment. Modern poetry continues to develop, and will no doubt continue to change as values, thought, and writing continue to change.

Poems can be among the most enlightening and uplifting texts for a person to read if they are looking to connect with the past, connect with other people, or try to gain an understanding of what is happening in their time.

5. In summary, the author has written this passage

    a. as a foreword that will introduce a poem in a book or magazine

    b. because she loves poetry and wants more people to like it

    c. to give a brief history of poems

    d. to convince students to write poems

6. The author organizes the paragraphs mainly by

    a. moving chronologically, explaining which types of poetry were common in that time

    b. talking about new types of poems each paragraph and explaining them a little

    c. focusing on one poet or group of people and the poems they wrote

    d. explaining older types of poetry so she can talk about modern poetry

7. The author's claim that poetry has been around "virtually from the time civilizations invented the written word" is supported by the detail that

    a. Beowulf is written in Old English, which is not really in use any longer

    b. epic poems told stories about heroes

    c. the Renaissance poets tried to copy Greek poets

    d. the Mesopotamians are credited with both inventing the word and writing "Epic of Gilgamesh"

8. According to the passage, it can be understood that the word "telling" means

    a. speaking

    b. significant

    c. soothing

    d. wordy

Questions 9 - 12 refer to the following passage.

Passage 3: "Winged Victory of Samothrace: the Statue of the Gods"

Students who read about the "Winged Victory of Samothrace" probably won't be able to picture what this statue looks like. However, almost anyone who knows a little about statues will recognize it when they see it: it is the statue of a winged woman who does not have arms or a head. Even the most famous pieces of art may be recognized by sight but not by name.

This iconic statue is of the Greek goddess Nike, who represented victory and was called Victoria by the Romans. The statue is sometimes called the "Nike of Samothrace." She was often displayed in Greek art as driving a chariot, and her speed or efficiency with the chariot may be what her wings symbolize. It is said that the statue was created around 200 BCE to celebrate a battle that was won at sea. Archaeologists and art historians believe the statue may have originally been part of a temple or other building, even one of the most important temples, Megaloi Theoi, just as many statues were used during that time.

"Winged Victory" does indeed appear to have had arms and a head when it was originally created, and it is unclear why they were removed or lost. Indeed, they have never been discovered, even with all the excavation that has taken place. Many speculate that one of her arms was raised and put to her mouth, as though she was shouting or calling out, which is consistent with the idea of her as a war figure. If the missing pieces were ever to be found, they might give Greek and art historians more of an idea of what Nike represented or how the statue was used. Learning about pieces of art through details like these can help students remember time frames or locations, as well as learn about the people who occupied them.

9. The author's title says the statue is "of the Gods" because

    a. the statue is very beautiful and even a god would find it beautiful

    b. the statue is of a Greek goddess, and gods were of primary importance to the Greek

    c. Nike lead the gods into war

    d. the statues were used at the temple of the gods and so it belonged to them

10. The third paragraph states that

a. the statue is related to war and was probably broken apart by foreign soldiers

b. the arms and head of the statue cannot be found because all the excavation has taken place

c. speculations have been made about what the entire statue looked like and what it symbolized

d. the statue has no arms or head because the sculptor lost them

11. The author's main purpose in writing this passage is to

a. demonstrate that art and culture are related and one can teach us about the other

b. persuade readers to become archeologists and find the missing pieces of the statue

c. teach readers about the Greek goddess Nike

d. to teach readers the name of a statue they probably recognize

12. The author specifies the indirect audience as "students" because

a. it is probably a student who is taking this test

b. most young people don't know much about art yet and most young people are students

c. students read more than people who are not students

d. the passage is based on a discussion of what we can learn about culture from art

Questions 13 - 16 refer to the following passage.

Passage 4: "Ways Characters Communicate in Theater"

Playwrights give their characters voices in a way that gives depth and added meaning to what happens on stage during their play. There are different types of speech in scripts that allow characters to talk with themselves, with other characters, and even with the audience.

It is very unique to theater that characters may talk "to themselves." When characters do this, the speech they give is called a soliloquy. Soliloquies are usually poetic, introspective, moving, and can tell audience members about the feelings, motivations, or suspicions of an individual character without that character having to reveal them to other characters on stage. "To be or not to be" is a famous soliloquy given by Hamlet as he considers difficult but important themes, such as life and death.

The most common type of communication in plays is when one character is speaking to another or a group of other characters. This is generally called dialogue, but can also be called monologue if one character speaks without being interrupted for a long time. It is not necessarily the most important type of communication, but it is the most common because the plot of the play cannot really progress without it.

Lastly, and most unique to theater (although it has been used somewhat in film) is when a character speaks directly to the audience. This is called an aside, and scripts usually specifically direct actors to do this. Asides are usually comical, an inside joke between the character and the audience, and very short. The actor will usually face the audience when delivering them, even if it's for a moment, so the audience can recognize this move as an aside.

All three of these types of communication are important to the art of theater, and have been perfected by famous playwrights like Shakespeare. Understanding these types of communication can help an audience member grasp what is artful about the script and action of a play.

13. According to the passage, characters in plays communicate to

    a. move the plot forward

    b. show the private thoughts and feelings of one character

    c. make the audience laugh

    d. add beauty and artistry to the play

14. When Hamlet delivers "To be or not to be," he can most likely be described as

    a. solitary

    b. thoughtful

    c. dramatic

    d. hopeless

15. The author uses parentheses to punctuate "although it has been used somewhat in film"

    a. to show that films are less important

    b. instead of using commas so that the sentence is not interrupted

    c. because parenthesis help separate details that are not as important

    d. to show that films are not as artistic

16. It can be understood that by the phrase "give their characters voices," the author means that

    a. playwrights are generous

    b. playwrights are changing the sound or meaning of characters' voices to fit what they had in mind

    c. dialogue is important in creating characters

    d. playwrights may be the parent of one of their actors and literally give them their voice

Questions 17 - 20 refer to the following passage.

Passage 5: "Women and Advertising"

Only in the last few generations have media messages been so widespread and so readily seen, heard, and read by so many people. Advertising is an important part of both selling and buying anything from soap to cereal to jeans. For whatever reason, more consumers are women than are men. Media message are subtle but powerful, and more attention has been paid lately to how these message affect women.

Of all the products that women buy, makeup, clothes, and other stylistic or cosmetic products are among the most popular. This means that companies focus their advertising on women, promising them that their product will make her feel, look, or smell better than the next company's product will. This competition has resulted in advertising that is more and more ideal and less and less possible for everyday women. However, because women do look to these ideals and the products they represent as how they can potentially become, many women have developed unhealthy attitudes about themselves when they have failed to become those ideals.

In recent years, more companies have tried to change advertisements to be healthier for women. This includes featuring models of more sizes and addressing a huge outcry against unfair tools such as airbrushing and photo editing. There is debate about what the right balance between real and ideal is, because fashion is also considered art and some changes are made to purposefully elevate fashionable products and signify that they are creative, innovative, and the work of individual people. Artists want their freedom protected as much as women do, and advertising agencies are often caught in the middle.

Some claim that the companies who make these changes are not doing enough. Many people worry that there are still not enough models of different sizes and different ethnicities. Some people claim that companies use this healthier type of advertisement not for the good of women, but because they would like to sell products to the women who are looking for these kinds of messages. This is also a hard balance to find: companies do need to make money, and women do need to feel respected.

While the focus of this change has been on women, advertising can also affect men, and this change will hopefully be a lesson on media for all consumers.

17. The second paragraph states that advertising focuses on women

    a. to shape what the ideal should be

    b. because women buy makeup

    c. because women are easily persuaded

    d. because of the types of products that women buy

18. According to the passage, fashion artists and female consumers are at odds because

    a. there is a debate going on and disagreement drives people apart

    b. both of them are trying to protect their freedom to do something

    c. artists want to elevate their products above the reach of women

    d. women are creative, innovative, individual people

19. The author uses the phrase "for whatever reason" in this passage to

    a. keep the focus of the paragraph on media messages and not on the differences between men and women

    b. show that the reason for this is unimportant

    c. argue that it is stupid that more women are consumers than men

    d. show that he or she is tired of talking about why media messages are important

20. This passage suggests that

    a. advertising companies are still working on making their messages better

    b. all advertising companies seek to be more approachable for women

    c. women are only buying from companies that respect them

    d. artists could stop producing fashionable products if they feel bullied

Questions 21 - 24 refer to the following passage.

Passage 6: "FDR, the Treaty of Versailles, and the Fourteen Points"

At the conclusion of World War I, both who had won the war and those who were forced to admit defeat welcomed the end of the war and anticipated that a peace treaty would be signed. The American president, Franklin Roosevelt, played an important part in proposing what the agreements should be and did so through his Fourteen Points.

World War I had begun in 1914 when an Austrian archduke was assassinated, leading to a domino effect that pulled the world's most powerful countries into war on a large scale. The war catalyzed the creation and use of deadly weapons that had not previously existed, resulting in a great loss of soldiers on both sides of the fighting. More than 9 million soldiers were killed.

The United States agreed to enter the war right before it ended, and they believed that its decision to become finally involved brought on the end of the war. FDR made it very clear that the U.S. was entering the war for moral reasons and had an agenda focused on world peace. The Fourteen Points were individual goals and ideas (focused on peace, free trade, open communication, and self reliance) that FDR wanted the power nations to strive for now that the war had concluded. He was optimistic and had many ideas about what could be accomplished through and during the post-war peace. However, FDR's fourteen points were poorly received when he presented them to the leaders of other world powers, many of whom wanted only to help their own countries and to punish the Germans for fueling the war, and they fell by the wayside. World War II was imminent, for Germany lost everything.

Some historians believe that the other leaders who participated in the Treaty of Versailles weren't receptive to the Fourteen Points because World War I was fought almost entirely on European soil, and the United States lost much less than did the other powers. FDR was in a unique position to help determine the fate of the war, but doing it on his own terms did not help accomplish his goals. This is only one historical example of how the United State has tried to use its power as an important country, but found itself limited because of geological or ideological factors.

21. The main idea of this passage is that

    a. World War I was unfair because no fighting took place in America

    b. World War II happened because of the Treaty of Versailles

    c. the power the United States has to help other countries also prevents it from helping other countries

    d. Franklin Roosevelt was one of the United States' smartest presidents

22. According to the second paragraph, World War I started because

    a. an archduke was assassinated

    b. weapons that were more deadly had been developed

    c. a domino effect of allies agreeing to help

    d. the world's most powerful countries were large

23. The author includes the detail that 9 million soldiers were killed

    a. to demonstrate why European leaders were hesitant to accept peace

    b. to show the reader the dangers of deadly weapons

    c. to make the reader think about which countries lost the most soldiers

    d. to demonstrate why World War II was imminent

24. According to this passage, it can be understood that the word catalyzed means

    i. a. analyzed

    j. b. sped up

    k. c. invented

    l. d. funded

Answer Key

Passage 1: "If You Have Allergies, You're Not Alone"

1. C
This question tests the reader's vocabulary skills. The uses of the negatives "but" and "less," especially right next to each other, may confuse readers into answering with choices A or D, which list words that are antonyms of "militant." Readers may also be confused by the comparison of healthy people with what is being described as an overly healthy person--both people are good, but the reader may look for which one is "worse" in the comparison, and therefore stray toward the antonyms. One key to understanding the meaning of "militant" if the reader is unfamiliar with it is to look at the root of the word; readers can then easily associate it with "military" and gain a sense of what the word signifies: defense (especially considered that the immune system defends the body). Choice C is correct over choice B because "militant" is an adjective, just as the words in C are, whereas the words in B are nouns.

2. C
This question tests the reader's understanding of function within writing. The other choices are details included surrounding the quoted text, and may therefore confuse the reader. A somewhat contradicts what is said earlier in the paragraph, which is that tests and treatments are improving, and probably doctors are along with them, but the paragraph doesn't actually mention doctors, and the subject of the question is the medicine. Choice B may seem correct to readers who aren't careful to understand that, while the author does mention the large number of people affected, the author is touching on the realities of living with allergies rather about the likelihood of curing all allergies. Similarly, while the author does mention the "balance" of the body, which is easily associated with "wholesome," the author is not really making an argument and especially is not making an extreme statement that allergy medicines should be outlawed. Again, because the article's tone is on living with allergies, choice C is an appropriate choice that fits with the title and content of the text.

3. B

This question tests the reader's inference skills. The text does not state who is doing the recommending, but the use of the "patients," as well as the general context of the passage, lends itself to the logical partner, "doctors," B. The author does mention the recommendation but doesn't present it as her own (i.e. "I recommend that"), so A may be eliminated. It may seem plausible that people with allergies (D) may recommend medicines or products to other people with allergies, but the text does not necessarily support this interaction taking place. Choice C may be selected because the EpiPen is specifically mentioned, but the use of the phrase "such as" when it is introduced is not limiting enough to assume the recommendation is coming from its creators.

4. D

This question tests the reader's global understanding of the text. Choice D includes the main topics of the three body paragraphs, and isn't too focused on a specific aspect or quote from the text, as the other questions are, giving a skewed summary of what the author intended. The reader may be drawn to Choice B because of the title of the passage and the use of words like "better," but the message of the passage is larger and more general than this.

Passage 2: "When a Poet Longs to Mourn, He Writes an Elegy"

5. C

This question tests the reader's summarization skills. The use of the word "actually" in describing what kind of people poets are, as well as other moments like this, may lead readers to selecting choice B or D, but the author is more information than trying to persuade readers. The author gives no indication that she loves poetry (B) or that people, students specifically (D), should write poems. Choice A is incorrect because the style and content of this paragraph do not match those of a foreword; forewords usually focus on the history or ideas of a specific poem to introduce it more fully and help it stand out against other poems. The author here focuses on several poems and gives broad statements. Instead, she tells a kind of story about poems, giving three very broad time periods in which to discuss them, thereby giving a brief history of poetry, as choice C states.

6. A
This question tests the reader's summarization skills. Key words in the topic sentences of each of the paragraphs ("oldest," "Renaissance," "modern") should give the reader an idea that the author is moving chronologically. The opening and closing sentence-paragraphs are broad and talk generally. Choice B seems reasonable, but epic poems are mentioned in two paragraphs, eliminating the idea that only new types of poems are used in each paragraph. Choice C is also easily eliminated because the author clearly mentions several different poets, groups of people, and poems. Choice D also seems reasonable, considering that the author does move from older forms of poetry to newer forms, but use of "so (that)" makes this statement false, for the author gives no indication that she is rushing (the paragraphs are about the same size) or that she prefers modern poetry.

7. D
This question tests the reader's attention to detail. The key word is "invented"--it ties together the Mesopotamians, who invented the written word, and the fact that they, as the inventors, also invented and used poetry. The other selections focus on other details mentioned in the passage, such as that the Renaissance's admiration of the Greeks (C) and that Beowulf is in Old English (A). Choice B may seem like an attractive answer because it is unlike the others and because the idea of heroes seems rooted in ancient and early civilizations.

8. B
This question tests the reader's vocabulary and contextualization skills. "Telling" is not an unusual word, but it may be used here in a way that is not familiar to readers, as an adjective rather than a verb in gerund form. Choice A may seem like the obvious answer to a reader looking for a verb to match the use they are familiar with. If the reader understands that the word is being used as an adjective and that choice A is a ploy, they may opt to select choice D, "wordy," but it does not make sense in context. Choice C can be

easily eliminated, and doesn't have any connection to the paragraph or passage. "Significant" (B) does make sense contextually, especially relative to the phrase "give insight" used later in the sentence.

Passage 3: "Winged Victory of Samothrace: the Statue of the Gods"

9. B
This question tests the reader's summarization skills. Choice A is a very broad statement that may or may not be true, and seems to be in context, but has nothing to do with the passage. The author does mention that the statue was probably used on a temple dedicated to the Greek gods (D), but in no way discusses or argues for the gods' attitude toward or claim on these temples or its faucets. Nike does indeed lead the gods into a war (the Titan war), as choice C suggests, but this is not mentioned by the passage and students who know this may be drawn to this answer but have not done a close enough analysis of the text that is actually in the passage. Choice B is appropriately expository, and connects the titular emphasis to the idea that the Greek gods are very important to Greek culture.

10. C
This question tests the reader's summarization skills. The test for question choice C is pulled straight from the paragraph, but is not word-for-word, so it may seem too obvious to be the right answer. The passage does talk about Nike being the goddess of war, as choice A states, but the third paragraph only touches on it and it is an inference that soldiers destroyed the statue, when this question is asking specifically for what the third paragraph actually stated. Choice B is also straight from the text, with a minor but key change: the inclusion of the words "all" and "never" are too limiting and the passage does not suggest that these limits exist. If a reader selects choice D, they are also making an inference that is misguided for this type of question. The paragraph does state that the arms and head are "lost" but does not suggest who lost them.

11. A
This question tests the reader's ability to recognize function

in writing. Choice B can be eliminated based on the purpose of the passage, which is expository and not persuasive. The author may or may not feel this way, but the passage does not show evidence of being argumentative for that purpose. Choices C and D are both details found in the text, but neither of them encompasses the entire message of the passage, which has an overall message of learning about culture from art and making guesses about how the two are related, as suggested by choice A.

12. D
This question tests the reader's ability to understand function within writing. Most of the possible selections are very general statements which may or may not be true. It probably is a student who is taking the test on which this question is featured (A), but the author makes no address to the test taker and is not talking to the audience in terms of the test. Likewise, it may also be true that students read more than adults (C), mandated by schools and grades, but the focus on the verb "read" in the first sentence is too narrow and misses the larger purpose of the passage; the same could be said for selection B. While all the statements could be true, choice D is the most germane, and infers the purpose of the passage without making assumptions that could be incorrect.

Passage 4: "Ways Characters Communicate in Theater"

13. D
This question tests the reader's summarization skills. The question is asking very generally about the message of the passage, and the title, "Ways Characters Communicate in Theater," is one indication of that. The other choices A, B, and C are all directly from the text, and therefore readers may be inclined to select one of them, but are too specific to encapsulate the entirety of the passage and its message.

14. B
The paragraph on soliloquies mentions "To be or not to be," and it is from the context of that paragraph that readers may understand that because "To be or not to be" is a soliloquy, Hamlet will be introspective, or thoughtful, while delivering it. It is true that actors deliver soliloquies alone,

and may be "solitary" (A), but "thoughtful" (B) is more true to the overall idea of the paragraph. Readers may choose C because drama and theater can be used interchangeably and the passage mentions that soliloquies are unique to theater (and therefore drama), but this answer is not specific enough to the paragraph in question. Readers may pick up on the theme of life and death and Hamlet's true intentions and select that he is "hopeless" (D), but those themes are not discussed either by this paragraph or passage, as a close textual reading and analysis confirms.

15. C
This question tests the reader's grammatical skills. Choice B seems logical, but parenthesis are actually considered to be a stronger break in a sentence than commas are, and along this line of thinking, actually disrupt the sentence more. Choices A and D make comparisons between theater and film that are simply not made in the passage, and may or may not be true. This detail does clarify the statement that asides are most unique to theater by adding that it is not completely unique to theater, which may have been why the author didn't chose not to delete it and instead used parentheses to designate the detail's importance (C).

16. C
This question tests the reader's vocabulary and contextualization skills. Choice A may or may not be true, but focuses on the wrong function of the word "give" and ignores the rest of the sentence, which is more relevant to what the passage is discussing. CHoices B and D may also be selected if the reader depends too literally on the word "give," failing to grasp the more abstract function of the word that is the focus of choice C, which also properly acknowledges the entirety of the passage and its meaning.

Passage 5: "Women and Advertising"

17. D
This question tests the reader's summarization skills. The other choices A, B, and C focus on portions of the second paragraph that are too narrow and do not relate to the specific portion of text in question. The complexity of the sentence may mislead students into selecting one of these

answers, but rearranging or restating the sentence will lead the reader to the correct answer. In addition, choice A makes an assumption that may or may not be true about the intentions of the company, choice B focuses on one product rather than the idea of the products, and choice C makes an assumption about women that may or may not be true and is not supported by the text.

18. B
This question tests reader's attention to detail. If a reader selects A, he or she may have picked up on the use of the word "debate" and assumed, very logically, that the two are at odds because they are fighting; however, this is simply not supported in the text. Choice C also uses very specific quotes from the text, but it rearranges them and gives them false meaning. The artists want to elevate their creations above the creations of other artists, thereby showing that they are "creative" and "innovative." Similarly, choice D takes phrases straight from the texts and rearranges and confuses them. The artists are described as wanting to be "creative, innovative, individual people," not the women.

19. A
This question tests reader's vocabulary and summarization skills. This phrase, used by the author, may seem flippant and dismissive if readers focus on the word "whatever" and misinterpret it as a popular, colloquial terms. In this way, the choices B and C may mislead the reader to selecting one of them by including the terms "unimportant" and "stupid," respectively. Choice D is a similar misreading, but doesn't make sense when the phrase is at the beginning of the passage and the entire passage is on media messages. Choice A is literarily and contextually appropriate, and the reader can understand that the author would like to keep the introduction focused on the topic the passage is going to discuss.

20. A
This question tests a reader's inference skills. The extreme use of the word "all" in choice B suggests that every single advertising company are working to be approachable, and while this is not only unlikely, the text specifically states that "more" companies have done this, signifying that they have not all participated, even if it's a possibility that they

may some day. The use of the limiting word "only" in choice C lends that answer similar problems; women are still buying from companies who do not care about this message, or those companies would not be in business, and the passage specifies that "many" women are worried about media messages, but not all. Readers may find choice D logical, especially if they are looking to make an inference, and while this may be a possibility, the passage does not suggest or discuss this happening. Choice A is correct based on specifically because of the relation between "still working" in the answer and "will hopefully" and the extensive discussion on companies struggles, which come only with progress, in the text.

Passage 6: "FDR, the Treaty of Versailles, and the Fourteen Points"

21. C
This question tests the reader's summarization skills. The entire passage is leading up to the idea that the president of the US may not have had grounds to assert his Fourteen Points when other countries had lost so much. Choice A is pretty directly inferred by the text, but it does not adequately summarize what the entire passage is trying to communicate. Choice B may also be inferred by the passage when it says that the war is "imminent," but it does not represent the entire message, either. The passage does seem to be in praise of FDR, or at least in respect of him, but it does not in any way claim that he is the smartest president, nor does this represent the many other points included. Choice C is then the obvious answer, and most directly relates to the closing sentences which it rewords.

22. C
This question tests the reader's attention to detail. The passage does state that choices A and B are true, and while those statements are in proximity to the explanation for why the war started, they are not the actual reason given. Choice D is a mix up of words used in the passage, which says that the largest powers were in play but not that this fact somehow started the war. The passage does make a direct statement that a domino effect started the war, supporting choice C as the correct answer.

23. A

This question tests the reader's understanding of functions in writing. Throughout the passage, it states that leaders of other nations were hesitant to accept generous or peaceful terms because of the grievances of the war, and the great loss of life was chief among these. While the passage does touch on the devastation of deadly weapons (B), the use of this raw, emotional fact serves a much larger purpose, and the focus of the passage is not the weapons. While readers may indeed consider who lost the most soldiers (C) when so many countries were involved and the inequalities of loss are mentioned in the passage, there is no discussion of this in the passage. Choice D is related to A, but choice A is more direct and relates more to the passage.

24. B

This question tests the reader's vocabulary skills. Choice A may seem appealing to readers because it is phonetically similar to "catalyzed," but the two are not related in any other way. Choice C makes sense in context, but if plugged into the sentence creates a redundancy that doesn't make sense. Choice D does also not make sense contextually, even if the reader may consider that funds were needed to create more weaponry, especially if it was advanced.

English Grammar Multiple-Choice

How to Answer English Grammar Multiple-Choice - Verb Tense

This tutorial is designed to help you answer English Grammar multiple-choice questions as well as a very quick refresher on verb tenses. It is assumed that you have some familiarity with the verb tenses covered here. If you find these questions difficulty or do not understand the tense construction, we recommend you seek out additional instruction.

Tenses Covered

1. Past Progressive
2. Present Perfect
3. Present Perfect Progressive
4. Present Progressive
5. Simple Future
6. Simple Future – "Going to" Form
7. Past Perfect Progressive
8. Future Perfect Progressive
9. Future Perfect
10. Future Progressive
11. Past Perfect

1. The Past Progressive Tense

How to Recognize This Tense

He *was running* very fast when he fell.

They *were drinking* coffee when he arrived.

About the Past Progressive Tense

This tense is used to speak of an action that was in progress in the past when another event occurred.

The action was unfolding at a point in the past.

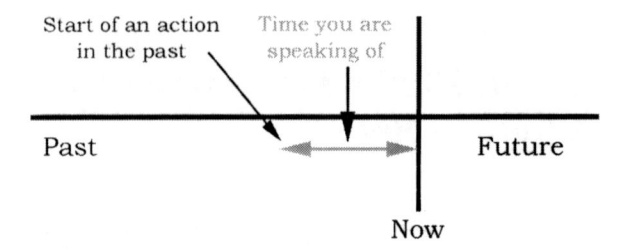

Past Progressive Tense Construction

This tense is formed by using the past tense of the verb "to be" plus the present participle of the main verb.

Sample Question

Bill _____ lunch when we arrived.

    a. will eat
    b. is eating
    c. eats
    d. was eating

How to Answer This Type of Question

1. First examine the question for clues about the time frame.

The sentence ends with "when we arrived," so we know the time frame is a point ("when") in the past (arrived).

The correct answer will refer to an ongoing action at a point of time in the past.

2. Examine the choices and eliminate any obviously incorrect answers.

Choice A is the future tense so we can eliminate.

Choice B is the present continuous so we can eliminate.

Choice C is present tense so we can eliminate.

Choice D refers to an action that takes place at a point of time in the past ("was eating").

2. The Present Perfect Tense
How to Recognize This Tense

I *have had* enough to eat.

We *have been* to Paris many times.

I *have known* him for five years.

I *have been* coming here since I was a child.

About the Present Perfect Tense

This tense expresses the idea that something happened (or didn't happen) at an unspecific time in the past until the present. The action happened at an unspecified time in the past. (If there is a specific time mentioned, the simple past tense is used.) It can be used for repeated action, accomplishments, changes over time and uncompleted action.

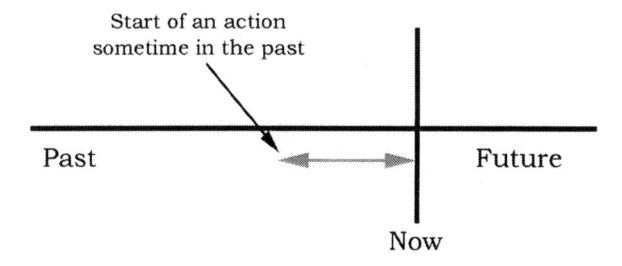

Present Perfect Tense Construction

It is also used with "for" and "since."

This tense is formed by using the present tense of the verb "to have" plus the past participle of the main verb.

Sample Question

I _____ these birds many times.

    a. am seeing
    b. will saw
    c. have seen
    d. have saw

How to Answer This Type of Question

1. First examine the question for clues about the time frame.

"Many times" tells us that the action is repeated and in the past.

2. Examine the choices and eliminate any obviously incorrect answers.

Choice A, "am seeing" is incorrect because it is a continuing action, i.e. in the present; it also doesn't use a form of 'have'.

Choice B is grammatically incorrect.

Choice C tells of something that has happened in the past and is now over. Best choice so far.

Choice D is grammatically incorrect.

3. The Present Perfect Progressive Tense
How to Recognize This Tense

We *have been seeing* a lot of rainy days.

I *have been reading* some very good books.

About the Present Perfect Progressive Tense

This tense expresses the idea that something happened (or didn't happen) in the relatively recent past, but <u>the action is not finished.</u> It is used to express the duration of the action.

NOTE: The present perfect speaks of an action that happened sometime in the past, but this action is finished. In the present perfect progressive tense, the action that started in the past is still going on.

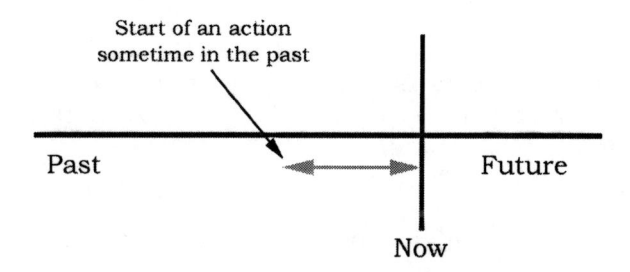

Present Perfect Progressive Tense Construction

This tense is formed by using the present tense of the verb "to have," plus "been," plus the present participle of the main verb.

Sample Question

Bill _____ there for two hours.

   a. sits
   b. sitting
   c. has been sitting
   d. will sat

How to Answer This Type of Question

1. First examine the question for clues about the time frame.

"For two hours" tells us that the action, "sits," is continuous up to now, and may continue into the future.

Note this sentence could also be the simple past tense,

Bill sat there for two hours.

Or the future tense,

Bill will sit there for two hours.

However, these are not among the options.

2. Examine the choices and eliminate any obviously incorrect answers.

Choice A is incorrect because it is the present tense.
Choice B is incorrect because it is the present continuous.
Choice C is correct. "Has been sitting" expresses a continuous action in the past that isn't finished.
Choice D is grammatically incorrect.

4. The Present Progressive Tense
How to Recognize This Tense

We *are having* a delicious lunch.

They *are driving* much too fast.

About the Present Progressive Tense

This tense is used to express what the action is <u>right now</u>. The action started in the recent past, and is continuing into the future.

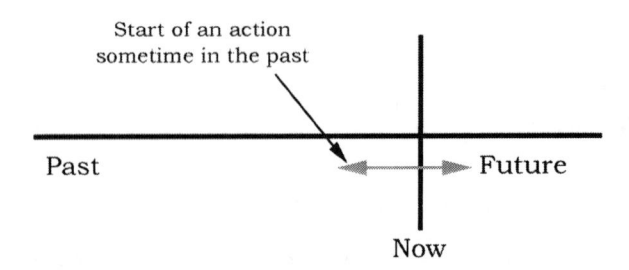

```
          Start of an action
          sometime in the past
                    |         |
                    ↓         |
    ─────────────────────────|──────────────
      Past          ←----+----→ Future
                         |
                         |
                        Now
```

Present Perfect Tense Construction

The Present Progressive Tense is formed by using the present tense of "to be" plus the present participle of the main verb.

Sample Question

She _____ very hard these days.

    a. works
    b. is working
    c. will work
    d. worked

How to Answer This Type of Question

1. First examine the question for clues about the time frame.

The end of the sentence includes "these days" which tell us the action started in the past, continues into the present, and may continue into the future.

2. Examine the choices and eliminate any obviously incorrect answers.

Choice A, the simple present is incorrect.
Choice B, "is working" is correct.
Check the other two choices just to be sure. Choice C is future tense, and choice D is past tense, so they can be eliminated.
The correct answer is choice B.

5. The Simple Future Tense
How to Recognize This Tense

I *will see* you tomorrow.
We *will drive* the car.

About the Simple Future Tense

This tense shows that the action will happen some time in the future.

```
                    Start of an action
                    sometime in the future
        |              ↙
————————|——————————————————————
        |    ◄┄┄┄┄┄►  Future
 Past   |
        |
       Now
```

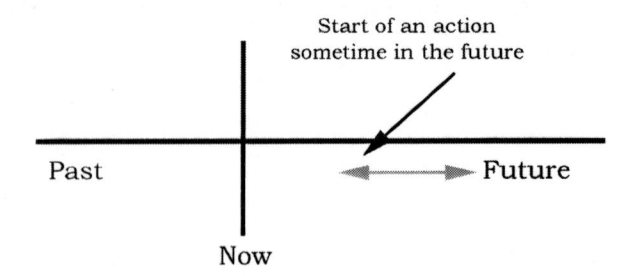

Simple Future Tense Construction

The tense is formed by using "will" plus the root form of the verb. (The root form of the verb is the infinitive without "to." Examples: read, swim.)

Sample Question

We _____ to Paris next year.

    a. went
    b. had been
    c. will go
    d. go

How to Answer This Type of Question

1. First examine the question for clues about the time frame.

The last two words of the sentence, "next year," clearly identify this sentence as referring to the future.

2. Examine the choices and eliminate any obviously incorrect answers.

Choice A is the past tense and can be eliminated.

Choice B is the past perfect tense and can be eliminated.

Choice D is the simple present and can be eliminated.

Choice C is the only one left and is the correct simple future tense.

6. The Simple Future Tense – The "Going to" Form

How to Recognize This Tense

I *am going to* see you tomorrow.

We *are going to* drive the car.

About the Simple Future Tense

This form of the future tense is used to show the intention of doing something in the future. (This is the strict grammatical meaning, but in daily speech, it is often used interchangeably with the simple future tense, the "will" form.)

The tense is formed by using the present conditional tense of "to go," plus the infinitive of the verb.

Sample Question

I _____ shopping in an hour.

    a. go
    b. have gone
    c. am going to go
    d. went

How to Answer This Type of Question

1. First examine the question for clues about the time frame.

"In an hour" clearly identifies the action as taking place in the future.

2. Examine the choices and eliminate any obviously incorrect answers.

Choice A is the simple present tense and can be eliminated.

Choice B is the past perfect and can be eliminated.

Choice C is the correct answer.

Choice D is the past tense and can be eliminated.

7. The Past Perfect Progressive Tense
How to Recognize This Tense

I *had been sleeping* for an hour when you phoned.

We *had been eating* our dinner when they all came into the dining room.

About the Past Perfect Progressive Tense

This tense is used to show that the action had been going on for a period of time in the past when another action, also in the past, occurred.

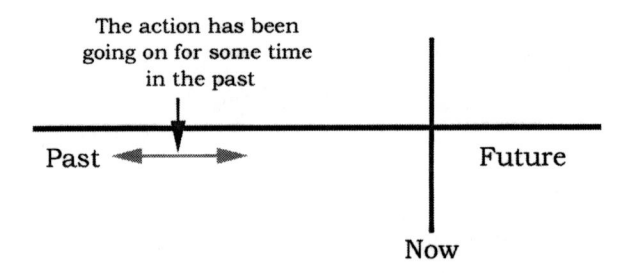

```
              The action has been
              going on for some time
                 in the past
                      |
                      ↓
     Past ←——————→              Future
                         |
                        Now
```

Past Perfect Tense Construction

The tense is formed by using the past perfect tense of the verb "to be" plus the present participle of the main verb.

Sample Question

How long _____ you _____ when I saw you?

    a. are ____ running
    b. had ____ running
    c. had ____ been running
    d. was ____ running

How to Answer This Type of Question

1. First examine the question for clues about the time frame.

"When I saw" tells us the sentence happened at a point of time ("when") in the past ("saw").

2. Examine the choices and eliminate any obviously incorrect answers.

Choice A, "are running" is incorrect and can be eliminated.

Choice B, "Had ___ running" is grammatically incorrect and can be eliminated.

Choice C is correct.

Choice D is grammatically incorrect so the answer is Choice C.

8. Future Perfect Progressive Tense
How to Recognize This Tense

I *will have been working* here for two years in March.

I *will have been driving* for four hours when I get there, so I will be tired.

About the Future Perfect Progressive Tense

This tense is used to show that the action continues up to a point of time in the future.

Future Prefect Progressive Tense Construction

This tense is formed by using the future perfect tense of "to be" plus the present participle of the main verb.

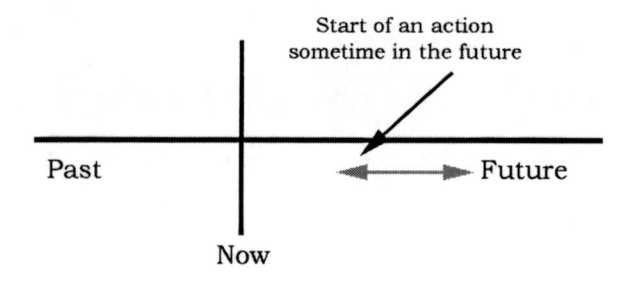

Sample Question

_____ you _____ all the time I am gone?

    a. have _____ been working
    b. will _____ have been working
    c. are _____ worked
    d. will _____ worked

How to Answer This Type of Question

1. First examine the question for clues about the time frame.

"All the time I am gone" refers to an action in the future ("time I am gone") and the action is progressive ("all the time"). The progressive action means the correct choice will be a verb tense that ends in "ing."

2. Examine the choices and eliminate any obviously incorrect answers.

Choice A, the past perfect, refers to a past continuous event and is also grammatically incorrect in the sentence, so choice A can be eliminated.

Choice B looks correct because it refers to an action will be going on for a period of time in the future.

Examine choices C and D just to be sure. Both choices are grammatically incorrect and can be eliminated. Choice B is the correct answer.

9. The Future Perfect Tense

How to Recognize This Tense

By next November, I *will have received* my promotion.

By the time he gets home, she is going *to have cleaned* the entire house.

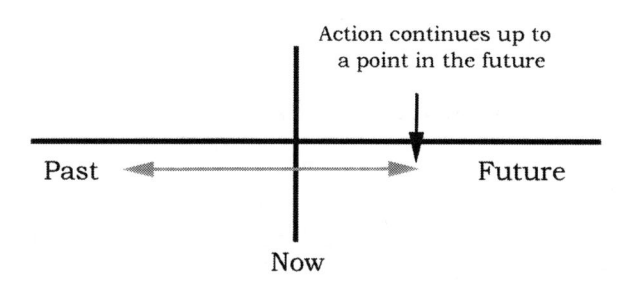

About the Future Perfect Tense

The future perfect tense expresses action in the future before another action in the future. This is the past in the future. For example:

He *will have prepared* dinner when she arrives.

Future Perfect Tense Construction

This tense is formed by "will + have + past participle."

Sample Question

They _____ their seats before the game begins.

    a. will have find
    b. will find
    c. will have found
    d. found

How to Answer This Type of Question

1. First examine the question for clues about the time frame.

This question could be several different tenses. The only clue about the time frame is "before the game begins," which refers to a specific point of time.

We know it isn't in the past, because "begins" is incorrect for the past tense. Similarly with the present. So the question is about something that happens in the future, before another event in the future.

2. Examine the choices and eliminate any obviously incorrect answers.

Choice A can be eliminated as incorrect.
Choice B looks good, so mark it and check the others before making a final decision.
Choice C is the past perfect and can be eliminated because the time frame is incorrect.
Choice D is the simple past tense and can be eliminated for the same reason.

10. Future Progressive Tense

How to Recognize This Tense

The teams *will be playing* soccer when we arrive.

At 3:45 the soccer fans *will be waiting* for the game to start at 4:00 o'clock

At 3:45 the soccer players *will be preparing* to play at 4:00 o'clock

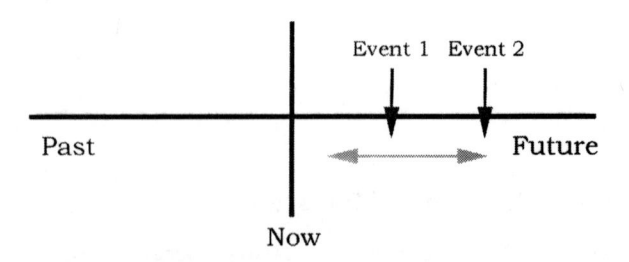

About the Future Progressive Tense

The future progressive tense talks about a continuing action in the future.

Future Progressive Tense Construction

will+ be + (root form) + ing = will be playing

Sample Question

Many excited fans _____ a bus to see the game at 4:00.

    a. catch
    b. catching
    c. have been catching
    d. will be catching

How to Answer This Type of Question

1. First examine the question for clues about the time frame.

"At 4:00," tells us the sentence is either in the past OR in the future.

2. Examine the choices and eliminate any obviously incorrect answers.

From the time frame of the sentence, the answer will be past or future tense.

Choice A is the present tense and can be eliminated.
Choice B is the present continuous tense and can be eliminated.
Choice C is the past perfect continuous and can be eliminated.
Choice D is the only one left. Quickly examining the tense, it is future progressive and is correct in the sentence.

11. The Past Perfect Tense
How to Recognize This Tense

The party *had* just *started* when the coach arrived.

We *had waited* for twenty minutes when the bus finally came.

About the Past Perfect

The past perfect tense talks about two events that happened in the past and establishes which event happened first.

Another example is, "We had eaten when he arrived."

The two events are "eat" and "he arrived." From the sentence above the past perfect tense tells us the first event, "eat" happened before the second event, "he arrived."

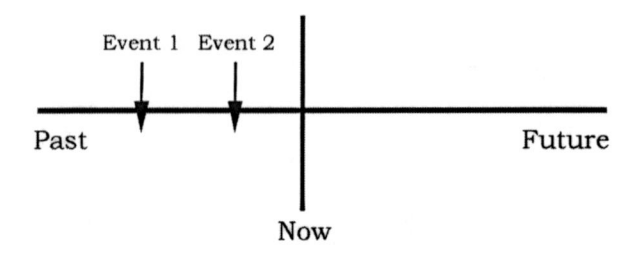

I had already eaten when my friends arrived.

Past Perfect Tense Construction

The past perfect is formed by "have" plus the past participle.

Sample Question

It was time to go home after they _____ the game.

    a. will win
    b. win
    c. had won
    d. wins

How to Answer This Type of Question

1. First examine the question for clues about the time frame.

"Was" tells us the sentence happened in the past. Also notice there are two events, "go home" and "after the game."

2. Examine the choices and eliminate any obviously incorrect answers.

Choice A is the future tense and can be eliminated. Choice B is the simple present and can be eliminated. Choice C is the past perfect and orders the two events in the past. Choice D is the present tense and incorrect and can be eliminated, so choice C is the correct answer.

Common English Usage Mistakes - A Quick Review

Like some parts of English grammar, usage is definitely going to be on the exam and there isn't any tricky strategies or shortcuts to help you get through this section.
Here is a quick review of common usage mistakes.

1. May and Might

'May' can act as a principle verb, which can express permission or possibility.

Examples:

Lets wait, the meeting may have started.
May I begin now?

'May' can act as an auxiliary verb, which an expresses a purpose or wish

Examples:

May you find favour in the sight of your employer.

May your wishes come true.
People go to school so that they may be educated.

The past tense of may is might.

Examples:

I asked if I might begin

'Might' can be used to signify a weak or slim possibility or polite suggestion.

Examples:

You might find him in his office, but I doubt it.
You might offer to help if you want to.

2. Lie and Lay

The verb lay should always take an object. The three forms of the verb lay are: laid, lay and laid.

The verb lie (recline) should not take any object. The three forms of the verb lie are: lay, lie and lain.

Examples:

Lay on the bed.
The tables were laid by the students.
Let the little kid lie.
The patient lay on the table.

The dog has lain there for 30 minutes.

Note: The verb lie can also mean "to tell a falsehood." This verb can appear in three forms: lied, lie, and lied. This is different from the verb lie (recline) mentioned above.

Examples:

The accused is fond of telling lies.
Did she lie?

3. Would and should

The past tense of shall is 'should', and so "should" generally follows the same principles as "shall."

The past tense of will is "would," and so "would" generally

follows the same principles as "will."

The two verbs 'would and should' can be correctly used interchangeably to signify obligation. The two verbs also have some unique uses too. Should is used in three persons to signify obligation.

Examples:

I should go after work.
People should do exercises everyday.
You should be generous.

"Would" is specially used in any of the three persons, to signify willingness, determination and habitual action.

Examples:

They would go for a test run every Saturday.
They would not ignore their duties.
She would try to be punctual.

4. Principle and Auxiliary Verbs

Two principle verbs can be used along with one auxiliary verb as long as the auxiliary verb form suits the two principle verbs.

Examples:

A number of people have been employed and some promoted.

A new tree has been planted and the old has been cut down.

Again note the difference in the verb form.

5. Can and Could

A. Can is used to express capacity or ability.

Examples:

I can complete the assignment today
He can meet up with his target.

B. Can is also used to express permission.

Examples:

Yes, you can begin

In the sentence below, "can" was used to mean the same thing as "may." However, the difference is that the word "can" is used for negative or interrogative sentences, while "may" is used in affirmative sentences to express possibility.

Examples:

They may be correct.   Positive sentence - use may.
Can this statement be correct? A question using "can."
It cannot be correct. Negative sentence using "can."

The past tense of can is could. It can serve as a principle verb when it is used to express its own meaning.

Examples:

In spite of the difficulty of the test, he could still perform well.
"Could" here is used to express ability.

6. Ought

The verb ought should normally be followed by the word to.

Examples:

I *ought to* close shop now.

The verb 'ought' can be used to express:

A. Desirability

You ought to wash your hands before eating. It is desirable to wash your hands.

B. Probability

She ought to be on her way back by now. She is probably on her way.

C. Moral obligation or duty

The government ought to protect the oppressed. It is the government's duty to protect the oppressed.

7. Raise and Rise

Rise
The verb rise means to go up, or to ascend.
The verb rise can appear in three forms, rose, rise, and risen. The verb should not take an object.

Examples:

The bird rose very slowly.
The trees rise above the house.
My aunt has risen in her career.

Raise
The verb raise means to increase, to lift up.
The verb raise can appear in three forms, raised, raise and raised.

Examples:

He raised his hand.
The workers requested a raise.
Do not raise that subject.

8. Past Tense and Past Participle

Pay attention to the proper use these verbs: sing, show, ring, awake, fly, flow, begin, hang and sink.

Mistakes usually occur when using the past participle and past tense of these verbs as they are often mixed up.

Each of these verbs can appear in three forms:
Sing, Sang, Sung.
Show, Showed, Showed/Shown.
Ring, Rang, Rung.
Awake, awoke, awaken
Fly, Flew, Flown.
Flow, Flowed, Flowed.
Begin, Began, Begun.
Hang, Hanged, Hanged (a criminal)
Hang, Hung, Hung (a picture)
Sink, Sank, Sunk.

Examples:

The stranger rang the door bell. (simple past tense)
I have rung the door bell already. (past participle - an action completed in the past)

The stone sank in the river. (simple past tense)
The stone had already sunk. (past participle - an action completed in the past)

The meeting began at 4:00.
The meeting has begun.

9. Shall and Will

When speaking informally, the two can be used interchangeably. In formal writing, they must be used correctly.

"Will" is used in the second or third person, while "shall" is used in the first person. Both verbs are used to express a time or even in the future.

Examples:

I shall, We shall (First Person)
You will (Second Person)
They will (Third Person)

This principle however reverses when the verbs are to be used to express threats, determination, command, willingness, promise or compulsion. In these instances, will is now used in first person and shall in the second and third person.

Examples:

I will be there next week, no matter what.
This is a promise, so the first person "I" takes "will."
You shall ensure that the work is completed.
This is a command, so the second person "you" takes "shall."

I will try to make payments as promised.
This is a promise, so the first person "I" takes "will."

They shall have arrived by the end of the day.
This is a determination, so the third person "they" takes shall.

Note
A. The two verbs, shall and will should not occur twice in the same sentence when the same future is being referred to

Example:

I shall arrive early if my driver is here on time.

B. Will should not be used in the first person when questions are being asked

Examples:

Shall I go ?
Shall we go?

Subject Verb Agreement

Verbs in any sentence must agree with the subject of the sentence both in person and number. Problems usually occur when the verb doesn't correspond with the right subject or the verb fails to match the noun close to it.

Unfortunately, there is no easy way around these principles - no tricky strategy or easy rule. You just have to memorize them.

Here is a quick review:

The verb to be, present (past)

Person	**Singular**	**Plural**
First	I am (was)	we are (were)
Second	you are (were)	you are (were)
Third	he, she, it is (was)	they are (were)

The verb to have, present (past)

Person	**Singular**	**Plural**
First	I have (had)	we have (had)
Second	you have (had)	you have (had)
Third	he, she, it has (had)	they have (had)

Regular verbs, e.g. to walk, present (past)

Person	**Singular**	**Plural**
First	I walk (walked)	we walk (walked)
Second	you walk (walked)	you walk (walked)
Third	he, she, it walks (walked)	they work (walked)

1. Every and Each

When nouns are qualified by "every" or "each," they take a singular verb even if they are joined by 'and'

Examples:

Each mother and daughter *was* a given separate test.
Every teacher and student *was* properly welcomed.

2. Plural Nouns

Nouns like measles, tongs, trousers, riches, scissors etc. are all plural.

Examples:

The trousers *are* dirty.
My scissors *have* gone missing.
The tongs *are* on the table.

3. With and As Well

Two subjects linked with "with" or "as well" should have a verb that matches the first subject.

Examples:

The pencil, with the papers and equipment, *is* on the desk.
David as well as Louis is coming.

4. Plural Nouns

The following nouns take a singular verb:

> politics, mathematics, innings, news, advice, summons, furniture, information, poetry, machinery, vacation, scenery

Examples:

The machinery *is* difficult to assemble
The furniture *has* been delivered
The scenery *was* beautiful

5. Single Entities

A proper noun in plural form that refers to a single entity requires a singular verb. This is a complicated way of saying; some things appear to be plural, but are really singular, or some nouns refer to a collection of things but the collection is really singular.

Examples:

The United Nations Organization *is* the decision maker in the matter.

Here the "United Nations Organization" is really only one "thing" or noun, but is made up of many "nations."

The book, "The Seven Virgins" *was* not available in the library.

Here there is only one book, although the title of the book is plural.

6. Specific Amounts are always singular

A plural noun that refers to a specific amount or quantity that is considered as a whole (dozen, hundred, score etc) requires a singular verb.

Examples:

60 minutes *is* quite a long time.
Here "60 minutes" is considered a whole, and therefore one item (singular noun).

The first million is the most difficult.

7. Either, Neither and Each are always singular

The verb is always singular when used with: either, each, neither, every one and many.
Examples:

Either of the boys *is* lying.
Each of the employees *has* been well compensated
Many a police officer *has* been found to be courageous
Every one of the teachers *is* responsible

8. Linking with Either, Or, and Neither match the second subject

Two subjects linked by "either," "or," "nor" or "neither" should have a verb that matches the second subject.

Examples:

Neither David nor Paul *will* be coming.
Either Mary or Tina *is* paying.

Note
If one of the subjects linked by "either," "or," "nor" or "neither" is in plural form, then the verb should also be in plural, and the verb should be close to the plural subject.

Examples:
Neither the mother *nor* her kids *have* eaten.
Either Mary *or* her *friends are* paying.

9. Collective Nouns are Plural

Some collective nouns such as poultry, gentry, cattle, vermin etc. are considered plural and require a plural verb.

Examples:

The *poultry are* sick.
The *cattle are* well fed.

Note
Collective nouns involving people can work with both plural and singular verbs.

Examples:

Nigerians are known to be hard working
Europeans live in Africa

10. Nouns that are Singular and Plural

Nouns like deer, sheep, swine, salmon etc. can be singular or plural and require the same verb form.

Examples:

The swine is feeding. (singular)
The swine are feeding. (plural)

The salmon is on the table. (singular)
The salmon are running upstream. (plural)

11. Collective Nouns are Singular

Collective nouns such as Army, Jury, Assembly, Committee, Team etc should carry a singular verb when they subscribe to one idea. If the ideas or views are more than one, then the verb used should be plural.

Examples:

The committee is in agreement in their decision.

The committee were in disagreement in their decision.
The jury has agreed on a verdict.

The jury were unable to agree on a verdict.

12. Subjects links by "and" are plural.

Two subjects linked by "and" always require a plural verb

Examples:

David and John are students.

Note
If the subjects linked by "and" are used as one phrase, or constitute one idea, then the verb must be singular

The color of his socks and shoe is black.
Here "socks and shoe" are two nouns, however the subject is "color" which is singular.

English Grammar and Usage Answer Sheet

	A B C D E		A B C D E
1	○ ○ ○ ○ ○	31	○ ○ ○ ○ ○
2	○ ○ ○ ○ ○	32	○ ○ ○ ○ ○
3	○ ○ ○ ○ ○	33	○ ○ ○ ○ ○
4	○ ○ ○ ○ ○	34	○ ○ ○ ○ ○
5	○ ○ ○ ○ ○	35	○ ○ ○ ○ ○
6	○ ○ ○ ○ ○	36	○ ○ ○ ○ ○
7	○ ○ ○ ○ ○	37	○ ○ ○ ○ ○
8	○ ○ ○ ○ ○	38	○ ○ ○ ○ ○
9	○ ○ ○ ○ ○	39	○ ○ ○ ○ ○
10	○ ○ ○ ○ ○	40	○ ○ ○ ○ ○
11	○ ○ ○ ○ ○	41	○ ○ ○ ○ ○
12	○ ○ ○ ○ ○	42	○ ○ ○ ○ ○
13	○ ○ ○ ○ ○	43	○ ○ ○ ○ ○
14	○ ○ ○ ○ ○	44	○ ○ ○ ○ ○
15	○ ○ ○ ○ ○	45	○ ○ ○ ○ ○
16	○ ○ ○ ○ ○	46	○ ○ ○ ○ ○
17	○ ○ ○ ○ ○	47	○ ○ ○ ○ ○
18	○ ○ ○ ○ ○	48	○ ○ ○ ○ ○
19	○ ○ ○ ○ ○	49	○ ○ ○ ○ ○
20	○ ○ ○ ○ ○	50	○ ○ ○ ○ ○
21	○ ○ ○ ○ ○	51	○ ○ ○ ○ ○
22	○ ○ ○ ○ ○	52	○ ○ ○ ○ ○
23	○ ○ ○ ○ ○	53	○ ○ ○ ○ ○
24	○ ○ ○ ○ ○	54	○ ○ ○ ○ ○
25	○ ○ ○ ○ ○	55	○ ○ ○ ○ ○
26	○ ○ ○ ○ ○	56	○ ○ ○ ○ ○
27	○ ○ ○ ○ ○	57	○ ○ ○ ○ ○
28	○ ○ ○ ○ ○	58	○ ○ ○ ○ ○
29	○ ○ ○ ○ ○	59	○ ○ ○ ○ ○
30	○ ○ ○ ○ ○	60	○ ○ ○ ○ ○

English Grammar Practice Questions

1. **Choose the sentence with the correct grammar.**

   a. The man was asked to come with his daughter and her test results.

   b. The man was asked to come with her daughter and her test results.

   c. The man was asked to come with her daughter and our test results.

   d. None of the above.

2. **Choose the sentence with the correct grammar.**

   a. Every doctor must come with his stethoscope

   b. Every doctor must come with their stethoscope

   c. Every doctor must come with our stethoscope

   d. None of the above.

3. **Choose the sentence with the correct grammar.**

   a. Each of them have to be given a ticket.

   b. Each of them is to be given a ticket.

   c. Each of them are to be given a ticket.

   d. None of the above.

4. **Choose the sentence with the correct grammar.**

   a. The scenery were breathtaking.

   b. The scenery was breathtaking.

   c. Both of the above

   d. None of the above

5. Choose the sentence with the correct grammar.

    a. Neither the teacher nor the student is left in class.
    b. Neither the teacher nor the student are left in class.
    c. Both of the above.
    d. None of the above.

6. Choose the sentence with the proper usage.

    a. The meeting may have started.
    b. The meeting might have started.
    c. Both of the above.
    d. None of the above.

7. Choose the sentence with the proper usage.

    a. He can be correct
    b. He could be correct
    c. He may be correct
    d. None of the above

8. Choose the sentence with the correct grammar.

    a. The vermin are to be exterminated.
    b. The vermin is to be exterminated.
    c. The vermin was to be exterminated.
    d. None of the above.

9. Choose the sentence with the correct grammar.

    a. The salmon has been cooked.
    b. The salmon have been cooked.
    c. Both of the above.
    d. None of the above.

10. Choose the sentence with the correct grammar.

    a. Many of the students came with their lunch box.

    b. Many of the students came with our lunch box.

    c. Many of the students came with his or her lunch box.

    d. None of the above.

11. Choose the sentence with the correct grammar.

    a. The driver and the cleaner were to be sacked.

    b. The driver and the cleaner are to be sacked.

    c. The driver and the cleaner is to be sacked.

    d. None of the above.

12. Choose the sentence with the correct grammar.

    a. Here are the names of people whom you should contact.

    b. Here are the names of people who you should contact.

    c. Both of the above.

    d. None of the above.

13. Choose the sentence with the proper usage.

    a. Christians believe that their lord have raised.

    b. Christians believe that their lord have risen.

    c. Christians believe that their lord have raise.

    d. None of the above.

14. Choose the sentence with the proper usage.

    a. I will be at the office by 9 a. m.

    b. I shall be at the office by 9 a. m.

    c. Both of the above.

    d. None of the above.

15. Choose the sentence with the correct grammar.

   a. The army are interested in buying the property.

   b. The army is interested in buying the property.

   c. The army were interested in buying the property.

   d. None of the above.

16. Choose the sentence with the correct grammar.

   a. The poultry is sold off yesterday.

   b. The poultry were sold off yesterday.

   c. The poultry was sold off yesterday.

   d. None of the above.

17. Choose the sentence with the correct grammar.

   a. Mark and Peter have stopped to each other.

   b. Mark and Peter have stopped to one another.

   c. Both of the above.

   d. None of the above.

18. Choose the sentence with the correct grammar.

   a. The teacher asked everybody is to submit his assignment by 9 a.m.

   b. The teacher asked everybody is to submit our assignment by 9 a.m.

   c. The teacher asked everybody is to submit their assignment by 9 a.m.

   d. None of the above.

19. Choose the sentence with the proper usage.

   a. I will ensure that you receive the proper reward.

   b. I shall ensure that you receive the proper reward.

   c. Both of the above.

   d. None of the above.

20. Choose the sentence with the proper usage.

a. He ought to be back by now.
b. He ought be back by now.
c. He ought come back by now.
d. None of the above.

21. Choose the sentence with the correct grammar.

a. The gentry were well taken off at the reception.
b. The gentry was well taken off at the reception.
c. The gentry are well taken off at the reception.
d. None of the above.

22. Choose the sentence with the correct grammar.

a. The deer are running for their lives.
b. The deer is running for their lives.
c. Both of the above.
d. None of the above.

23. Choose the sentence with the correct grammar.

a. His measles is getting better.
b. His measles are getting better.
c. Both of the above.
d. None of the above.

24. Choose the sentence with the correct grammar.

a. Each player gets a locker to keep their personal things.
b. Each player gets a locker to keep his personal things.
c. Each player gets a locker to keep our personal things.
d. None of the above.

25. Choose the sentence with the proper usage.

  a. The tables were laid by the students.
  b. The tables were lay by the students.
  c. The tables were lie by the students.
  d. None of the above.

26. Choose the sentence with the correct grammar.

  a. The teachers and the student are standing in the hall.
  b. The teachers and the student is standing in the hall.
  c. Both of the above.
  d. None of the above.

27. Choose the sentence with the proper usage.

  a. Shall I give my speech now?
  b. Will I give my speech now?
  c. Both of the above.
  d. None of the above.

28. Choose the sentence with the correct grammar.

  a. Any girl that fails the test loses their admission.
  b. Any girl that fails the test loses our admission.
  c. Any girl that fails the test loses her admission.
  d. None of the above.

29. Choose the sentence with the proper usage.

  a. The dog has lay there for 30 minutes.
  b. The dog has lie there for 30 minutes.
  c. The dog has lain there for 30 minutes.
  d. None of the above.

30. Choose the sentence with the correct grammar.

  a. The sad news were delivered this morning.

  b. The sad news are delivered this morning.

  c. The sad news was delivered this morning.

  d. None of that above.

31. Choose the sentence with the proper usage.

  a. He told him to raised it up.

  b. He told him to raise it up.

  c. He told him to rise it up.

  d. None of the above.

32. Choose the sentence with the correct grammar.

  a. Neither of them came with their bicycle.

  b. Neither of them came with his bicycle.

  c. Neither of them came with our bicycle.

  d. None of the above.

33. Choose the sentence with the proper usage.

  a. A number of people have been employed and others promoted.

  b. A number of people have been sacked and others have been employed.

  c. A number of people sacked and others have been promoted.

  d. None of the above.

34. Choose the sentence with the correct grammar.

　　a. Politics were a dirty game.
　　b. Politics is a dirty game.
　　c. Politics are a dirty game.
　　d. None of the above.

35. Choose the sentence with the correct grammar.

　　a. The members of the team were asked to discuss with each other.
　　b. The members of the team were asked to discuss with one another.
　　c. Both of the above.
　　d. None of the above.

36. Choose the sentence with the correct grammar.

　　a. Their wages is been cut by half.
　　b. Their wages has been cut by half.
　　c. Their wages have been cut by half.
　　d. None of the above.

37. Choose the sentence with the proper usage.

　　a. In spite of the BAD weather yesterday, he can still attend the party.
　　b. In spite of the BAD weather yesterday, he could still attend the party.
　　c. In spite of the BAD weather yesterday, he may still attend the party.
　　d. None of the above.

English Grammar and Usage

38. Choose the sentence with the correct grammar.

a. The World Health Organization (WHO) were meeting by January.

b. The World Health Organization (WHO) are meeting by January.

c. The World Health Organization (WHO) is meeting by January.

d. None of the above.

39. Choose the sentence with the correct grammar.

a. Everyone was asked to raise their hand.

b. Everyone was asked to raise our hand.

c. Everyone was asked to raise her hand.

d. None of the above.

40. Choose the sentence with the proper usage.

a. They never and never will disobey the rules.

b. They never have and never will disobey the rules.

c. Both of the above.

d. None of the above.

41. Choose the sentence with the correct grammar.

a. Neither of them were coming along.

b. Neither of them is coming along.

c. Neither of them are coming along.

d. None of the above.

42. Choose the sentence with the correct grammar.

a. Everyone are to wear a black tie.

b. Everyone have to wear a black tie.

c. Everyone has to wear a black tie.

d. None of the above.

43. Choose the sentence with the proper usage.

    a. She was nodding her head, her hips are swaying.

    b. She was nodding her head, her hips is swaying.

    c. She was nodding her head, her hips were swaying.

    d. None of the above

44. Choose the sentence with the correct grammar.

    a. The broken furniture has been replaced.

    b. The broken furniture have been replaced.

    c. The broken furniture is been replaced.

    d. None of the above.

45. Choose the sentence with the correct grammar.

    a. Who would be giving the opening address?

    b. Whom will be giving the opening address?

    c. Both of the above.

    d. None of the above.

46. Choose the sentence with the correct grammar.

    a. 15 minutes is all the time you have to complete the test.

    b. 15 minutes are all the time you have to complete the test.

    c. Both of the above.

    d. None of the above.

47. Choose the sentence with the proper usage.

    a. They will have to retire when they reach 60 years of age.

    b. They shall have to retire when they reach 60 years of age.

    c. Both of the above.

    d. None of the above.

English Grammar and Usage

48. Choose the sentence with the correct grammar.

    a. The scissors are on the table
    b. The scissors is on the table
    c. Both of the above
    d. None of the above

49. Choose the sentence with the correct grammar.

    a. The new machinery were working at full capacity
    b. The new machinery are working at full capacity
    c. The new machinery is working at full capacity
    c. None of the above

50. Choose the sentence with the correct grammar.

    a. Either Paul or Mary is the thief
    b. Either Paul or Mary are the thief
    c. Either Paul or Mary were the thief
    d. None of the above

Answer Key

1. A
A pronoun should conform to its antecedent in gender, number and person.

2. A
Words such as neither, each, many, either, every, everyone, everybody and any should take a singular pronoun.

3. B
Use a singular verb with either, each, neither, everyone and many.

4. B
Always use the singular verb form for nouns like politics, wages, mathematics, innings, news, advice, summons, furniture, information, poetry, machinery, vacation, scenery etc.

5. A
When two subjects are linked by "either," "or," "nor," or "neither," use a verb that matches the second subject.

6. A
The verb "may" is used to express possibility or permission. Might is the past tense of may. In casual conversation, may and might are often used interchangeably, however, although it is grammatically incorrect.

7. C
Although the CAN could be used to mean the same thing as the word MAY, the difference is that the word can is used for negative or interrogative sentences, while may is used in affirmative sentences to express possibility.

8. A
Use the plural verb form with collective nouns such as poultry, gentry, cattle, vermin etc.

9. C
Nouns like deer, sheep, swine, salmon etc can take a

singular or plural verb depending if they are used in their singular or plural form.

10. C
Words such as neither, each, many, either, every, everyone, everybody and any should take a singular pronoun.

11. B
Two subjects linked by "and" with the use of the article "the" affects the nature of the verb to be used and so a plural verb is required.

12. A
Use "whom" in the objective case, and use "who" a subjective case.

13. B
The verb rise ('to go up', 'to ascend.') can appear in three forms, rise, rose, and risen. The verb should not take an object.

14. B
"Will" is used in the second or third person (they, he, she and you), while "shall" is used in the first person (I and we). Both verbs are used to express futurity. In common usage and everyday conversation, however, they can be interchanged.

15. B
Use the singular verb form with collective nouns such as army, jury, assembly, committee, team etc. when they subscribe to one idea. If the ideas or views are more than one, use the plural form.

16. B
Use the plural verb form with collective nouns such as poultry, gentry, cattle, vermin etc.

17. A
When you use 'each other' it should be used for two things or people. When you use 'one another' it should be used for things and people above two

18. A
Words such as neither, each, many, either, every, everyone, everybody and any should take a singular pronoun.

19. B
"Shall" is used in the second or third person (they, he, she and you), while "will" is used in the first person (I and we) when they are used to express threats, determination, command, willingness, promise or compulsion.

20. A
The verb "ought" can be used to express desirability, duty and probability. The verb is usually followed by "to."

21. A
Use the plural verb form with collective nouns such as poultry, gentry, cattle, vermin etc.

22. A
Nouns like deer, sheep, swine, salmon etc can take a singular or plural verb depending if they are used in their singular or plural form.

23. B
Use a plural verb for nouns like measles, tongs, trousers, riches, scissors etc.

24. B
Words such as neither, each, many, either, every, everyone, everybody and any should take a singular pronoun.

25. A
The verb LAY should always take an object. Here the subject is the table. The three forms of the verb lay are: lay, laid and laid. The sentence above is in past tense.

26. A
When two subjects are linked with "with" or "as well," use the verb form that matches the first subject.

27. A
"Will" is used in the second or third person (they, he, she and you), while "shall" is used in the first person (I and we)

when questions are asked.

28. C
Words such as neither, each, many, either, every, everyone, everybody and any should take a singular pronoun.

29. C
The verb lie (recline) should not take an object. The three forms of the verb lie are: l lie, lay and lain. The sentence above is in past tense.

30. C
Always use the singular verb form for nouns like politics, wages, mathematics, innings, news, advice, summons, furniture, information, poetry, machinery, vacation, scenery etc.

31. B
The verb raise ('to increase', 'to lift up.') can appear in three forms, raise, raised and raised.

32. B
Use a singular pronoun with words such as neither, each, many, either, every, everyone, everybody and any. Here we are assuming that the subject is male, and so use "his." The subject could be female, in which case we would use "her," however that is not a choice here.

33. B
Two principal verbs can be used along with one auxiliary verb as long as the auxiliary verb form suits the two principal verbs.

34. B
Always use the singular verb form for nouns like politics, wages, mathematics, innings, news, advice, summons, furniture, information, poetry, machinery, vacation, scenery etc.

35. B
When you use 'each other' it should be used for two things or people. When you use 'one another' it should be used for things and people above two.

36. C
Always use the singular verb form for nouns like politics, wages, mathematics, innings, news, advice, summons, furniture, information, poetry, machinery, vacation, scenery etc.

37. B
Use "could," the past tense of "can" to express ability or capacity.

38. C
Use a singular verb with a proper noun in plural form that refers to a single entity. Here the "The World Health Organization" is a single entity, although it is made up on many members.

39. C
Words such as neither, each, many, either, every, everyone, everybody and any should take a singular pronoun. Here we are assuming that the subject is female, and so use "her." The subject could be male, in which case we would use "his," however that is not one of the choices.

40. B
One principal verb can be used correctly with two auxiliary verbs as long as the form of principal verb used suits the two auxiliary verbs.

41. B
Use a singular verb with either, each, neither, everyone and many.

42. C
Use a singular verb with either, each, neither, everyone and many.

43. C
A verb can fit any of the two subjects in a compound sentence as long as the verb form agrees with that subject.

44. A
Always use the singular verb form for nouns like politics, wages, mathematics, innings, news, advice, summons,

furniture, information, poetry, machinery, vacation, scenery etc.

45. A
Use "whom" in the objective case, and use "who" a subjective case.

46. A
Use a singular verb with a plural noun that refers to a specific amount or quantity that is considered as a whole (dozen, hundred score etc).

47. A
Will is used in the second or third person (they, he, she and you), while shall is used in the first person (I and we). Both verbs are used to express futurity.

48. A
Use a plural verb for nouns like measles, tongs, trousers, riches, scissors etc.

49. C
Always use the singular verb form for nouns like politics, wages, mathematics, innings, news, advice, summons, furniture, information, poetry, machinery, vacation, scenery etc.

50. A
Use a singular verb with either, each, neither, everyone and many.

How to Improve your Vocabulary

VOCABULARY TESTS CAN BE DAUNTING WHEN YOU THINK OF THE ENORMOUS NUMBER OF WORDS THAT MIGHT COME UP IN THE EXAM. As the exam date draws near, your anxiety will grow because you know that no matter how many words you memorize, chances are, you will still remember so few, and there are so many more to memorize! Here are some tips which you can use to hurdle the big words that may come up in your exam without having to open the dictionary and memorize all the words known to humankind.

Build up and tear apart the big words. Big words, like many other things, are composed of small parts. Some words are made up of many other words. A man who lifts weights for example, is a weight lifter. Words are also made up of word parts called prefixes, suffixes and roots. Often times, we can see the relationship of different words through these parts. A person who is skilled with both hands is ambidextrous. A word with double meaning is ambiguous. A person with two conflicting emotions is ambivalent. Two words with synonymous meanings often have the same root. Bio, a root word derived from Latin is used in words like biography meaning to write about a person's life, and biology meaning the study of living organisms.

- **Words with double meanings.** Did you know that the word husband not only means a man married to a woman, but also thrift or frugality? Sometimes, words have double meanings. The dictionary meaning, or the denotation of a word is sometimes different from the way we use it or its connotation.

- **Read widely, read deeply and read daily.** The best way to expand your vocabulary is to familiarize yourself with as many words as possible through reading. By reading, you are able to remember words in a proper context and thus, remember its meaning or at the very least, its use. Reading widely would help you get acquainted with words you may never use every day. This is the best strategy without doubt. However, if you are studying for an exam next week, or even tomorrow, it isn't much help! Below you will find a range of different ways to learn new words quickly and efficiently.

- **Remember.** Always remember that big words are easy to understand when divided into smaller parts, and the smaller words will often have several other meanings aside from the one you already know. Below is an extensive list of root or stem words, followed by one hundred questions to help you learn word stems.

Here are suggested effective ways to help you improve your vocabulary.

- **Be Committed To Learning New Words**. To improve your vocabulary you need to make a commitment to learn new words. Commit to learning at least a word or two a day. You can also get new words by reading books, poems, stories, plays and magazines. Expose yourself to more language to increase the number of new words that you learn.

- **Learn Practical Vocabulary**. As much as possible, learn vocabulary that is associated with what you do and that you can use regularly. For example learn words related to your profession or hobby. Learn as much vocabulary as you can in your favorite subjects.

- **Use New Words Frequently**. As soon as you learn a new word start using it and do so frequently. Repeat it when you are alone and try to use the word as often as you can with people you talk to. You can also use flashcards to practice new words that you learn.

- **Learn the Proper Usage.** If you do not understand the proper usage, look it up and make sure you have it right.

- **Use a Dictionary**. When reading textbooks, novels

or assigned readings, keep the dictionary nearby. Also learn how to use online dictionaries and WORD dictionary. As soon as you come across a new word, check for its meaning. If you cannot do so immediately, then you should right it down and check it as soon as possible. This will help you understand what the word means and exactly how best to use it.

- **Learn Word Roots, Prefixes and Suffixes.** English words are usually derived from suffixes, prefixes and roots, which come from Latin, French or Greek. Learning the root or origin of a word helps you easily understand the meaning of the word and other words that are derived from the root. Generally, if you learn the meaning of one root word, you will understand two or three words. See our List of Stem Words below. This is a great two-for-one strategy. Most prefixes, suffixes, roots and stems are used in two, three or more words, so if you know the root, prefix or suffix, you can guess the meaning of many words.

- **Synonyms and Antonyms**. Most words in the English language have two or three (at least) synonyms and antonyms. For example, "big," in the most common usage, has about seventy-five synonyms and an equal number of antonyms. Understanding the relationships between these words and how they all fit together gives your brain a framework, which makes them easier to learn, remember and recall.

- **Use Flash Cards**. Flash cards are one of the best ways to memorize things. They can be used anywhere and anytime, so you can make use of odd free moments waiting for the bus or waiting in line. Make your own or buy commercially prepared flash cards, and keep them with you all the time.

- **Make word lists.** Learning vocabulary, like learning many things, requires repetition. Keep a new words journal in a separate section or separate notebook. Add any words that you look up in the dictionary, as well as from word lists. Review your word lists regularly.

Photocopying or printing off word lists from the Internet or handouts is not the same. Actually writing out the word and a few notes on the definition is an important process for imprinting the word in your brain. Writing out the word and definition in your New Word Journal, forces you to concentrate and focus on the new word. Hitting PRINT or pushing the button on the photocopier does not do the same thing.

Meaning in Context Answer Sheet

1. Ⓐ Ⓑ Ⓒ Ⓓ 21. Ⓐ Ⓑ Ⓒ Ⓓ
2. Ⓐ Ⓑ Ⓒ Ⓓ 22. Ⓐ Ⓑ Ⓒ Ⓓ
3. Ⓐ Ⓑ Ⓒ Ⓓ 23. Ⓐ Ⓑ Ⓒ Ⓓ
4. Ⓐ Ⓑ Ⓒ Ⓓ 24. Ⓐ Ⓑ Ⓒ Ⓓ
5. Ⓐ Ⓑ Ⓒ Ⓓ 25. Ⓐ Ⓑ Ⓒ Ⓓ
6. Ⓐ Ⓑ Ⓒ Ⓓ 26. Ⓐ Ⓑ Ⓒ Ⓓ
7. Ⓐ Ⓑ Ⓒ Ⓓ 27. Ⓐ Ⓑ Ⓒ Ⓓ
8. Ⓐ Ⓑ Ⓒ Ⓓ 28. Ⓐ Ⓑ Ⓒ Ⓓ
9. Ⓐ Ⓑ Ⓒ Ⓓ 29. Ⓐ Ⓑ Ⓒ Ⓓ
10. Ⓐ Ⓑ Ⓒ Ⓓ 30. Ⓐ Ⓑ Ⓒ Ⓓ
11. Ⓐ Ⓑ Ⓒ Ⓓ 31. Ⓐ Ⓑ Ⓒ Ⓓ
12. Ⓐ Ⓑ Ⓒ Ⓓ 32. Ⓐ Ⓑ Ⓒ Ⓓ
13. Ⓐ Ⓑ Ⓒ Ⓓ 33. Ⓐ Ⓑ Ⓒ Ⓓ
14. Ⓐ Ⓑ Ⓒ Ⓓ 34. Ⓐ Ⓑ Ⓒ Ⓓ
15. Ⓐ Ⓑ Ⓒ Ⓓ 35. Ⓐ Ⓑ Ⓒ Ⓓ
16. Ⓐ Ⓑ Ⓒ Ⓓ 36. Ⓐ Ⓑ Ⓒ Ⓓ
17. Ⓐ Ⓑ Ⓒ Ⓓ 37. Ⓐ Ⓑ Ⓒ Ⓓ
18. Ⓐ Ⓑ Ⓒ Ⓓ 38. Ⓐ Ⓑ Ⓒ Ⓓ
19. Ⓐ Ⓑ Ⓒ Ⓓ 39. Ⓐ Ⓑ Ⓒ Ⓓ
20. Ⓐ Ⓑ Ⓒ Ⓓ 40. Ⓐ Ⓑ Ⓒ Ⓓ

Meaning in Context

Meaning in context is a powerful tool for learning vocabulary. Essentially, you make an educated guess of the meaning from the context of the sentence. With meaning in context questions, also called sentence completion, you don't have to know the exact meaning - just an approximate meaning to answer the question.

This is also true is when reading. Sometimes it is necessary to know the exact meaning. Other times, the exact meaning is not important and you can make an educated guess from the context and continue reading.

The meaning in context exercises below give you practice making guesses about the meaning.

Directions: For each of the questions below, choose the word with the meaning best suited to the sentence based on the context.

1. When Joe broke his _____ in a skiing accident, his entire leg was in a cast.

    a. Ankle

    b. Humerus

    c. Wrist

    d. Femur

2. Alan had to learn the _____ system of numbering when his family moved to Great Britain.

    a. American

    b. Decimal

    c. Metric

    d. Fingers and toes

3. After Lisa's aunt had her tenth child, Lisa found that she had more than twenty _____ .

    a. Uncles

    b. Friends

    c. Stepsisters

    d. Cousins

4. Although he had flown many times, this was his first flight in a _____ .

    a. Helicopter

    b. Kite

    c. Train

    d. Subway car

5. George is very serious about his _____ , and recently joined the American Scholastic Association.

    a. Schoolwork

    b. Cooking

    c. Travelling

    d. Athletics

6. She was a rabid Red Sox fan, attending every game, and demonstrating her _____ by cheering more loudly than anyone else.

    a. Knowledge

    b. Boredom

    c. Commitment

    d. Enthusiasm

7. When Craig's dog was struck by a car, he rushed his pet to the _____.

    a. Emergency room

    b. Doctor

    c. Veterinarian

    d. Podiatrist

8. After she received her influenza vaccination, Nan thought that she was _____ to the common cold.

    a. Immune

    b. Susceptible

    c. Vulnerable

    d. At risk

9. Paul's rose bushes were being destroyed by Japanese beetles, so he invested in a good _____.

    a. Fungicide

    b. Fertilizer

    c. Sprinkler

    d. Pesticide

10. The last time that the crops failed, the entire nation experienced months of _____.

    a. Famine

    b. Harvest

    c. Plenitude

    d. Disease

11. Because of a pituitary dysfunction, Karl lacked the necessary _____ to grow as tall as his father.

    a. Glands

    b. Hormones

    c. Vitamins

    d. Testosterone

12. Because of its colorful fall _____ , the maple is my favorite tree.

    a. Growth

    b. Branches

    c. Greenery

    d. Foliage

13. When Mr. Davis returned from southern Asia, he told us about the _____ that sometimes swept the area, bringing torrential rain.

    a. Monsoons

    b. Hurricanes

    c. Blizzards

    d. Floods

14. Is it true that _____ always grows on the north side of trees?

    a. Lichens

    b. Moss

    c. Ferns

    d. Ground cover

15. You can _____ some fires by covering them with dirt, while others require foam or water.

    a. Extinguish
    b. Distinguish
    c. Ignite
    d. Lessen

16. Through the use of powerful fans that circulate the heat over the food, _____ ovens work very efficiently.

    a. Microwave
    b. Broiler
    c. Convection
    d. Pressure

17. Because of the growing use of _____ as a fuel, corn production has greatly increased.

    a. Alcohol
    b. Ethanol
    c. Natural gas
    d. Oil

18. In heavily industrialized areas, the air pollution causes many _____ diseases.

    a. Respiratory
    b. Cardiac
    c. Alimentary
    d. Circulatory

19. Because hydroelectric power is a _____ source of energy, its use is considered a green energy.

    a. Significant

    b. Disposable

    c. Renewable

    d. Reusable

20. The process required the use of highly _____ liquids, so fire extinguishers were everywhere in the factory.

    a. Erratic

    b. Combustible

    c. Inflammable

    d. Neutral

21. I still don't know exactly. That isn't _____ evidence.

    a. Undeterred

    b. Unrelenting

    c. Unfortunate

    d. Conclusive

22. He could manipulate the coins in his fingers very _____.

    a. Brazenly

    b. Eloquently

    c. Boisterously

    d. Deftly

23. His investment scheme _____ many serious investors, who lost money.

    a. Helped

    b. Vindicated

    c. Duped

    d. Reproved

24. When we go to a party, we always _____ a driver.

    a. Feign

    b. Exploit

    c. Dote

    d. Designate

25. This new evidence should _____ any doubts.

    a. Dispel

    b. Dispense

    c. Evaluate

    d. Diverse

26. She went to Asia on $10 a day – her _____ travelling plans are amazing.

    a. Frothy

    b. Frugal

    c. Fraught

    d. Focal

27. My grandmother's house is full or trinkets and ornaments. She is always buying _____ .

    a. Collectibles

    b. Baubles

    c. China

    d. Crystal

28. I am finally out of debt! I paid off all of my _____ .

    a. Debtors

    b. Defendants

    c. Accounts Receivable

    d. Creditors

29. I love listening to his speeches. He has a gift for _____ .

    a. Oratory

    b. Irony

    c. Jargon

    d. None of the above

30. The warehouse went bankrupt so all of the furniture has to be _____ .

    a. Dissected

    b. Liquidated

    c. Destroyed

    d. Bought

31. He sold the property when he didn't even own it. The whole thing was a _____.

    a. Hoax

    b. Feign

    c. Defile

    d. Default

32. The repair really isn't working. Those parts you replaced are _____.

    a. Despondent

    b. Illusive

    c. Deficient

    d. Granular

33. Just because she is supervisor, doesn't mean we have to _____ in front of her.

    a. Foible

    b. Grovel

    c. Humiliate

    d. Indispose

34. That noise is _____ ! It is driving me crazy.

    a. Loud

    b. Intolerable

    c. Frivolous

    d. Fictitious

35. Her inheritance was a good size and included many _____.

    a. Heirlooms

    b. Perchance

    c. Cynical

    d. Lateral

36. I see that sign everywhere. It is much more _____ than I thought.

    a. Prelude
    b. Prevalent
    c. Ratify
    d. Rational

37. Her attitude was very casual and _____.

    a. Idle
    b. Nonchalant
    c. Portly
    d. Portend

38. The machine _____ the rock into ore.

    a. Quells
    b. Pulverizes
    c. Eradicates
    d. Segments

39. The water in the pond has been sitting for so long it is _____.

    a. Stagnant
    b. Sediment
    c. Stupor
    d. Residue

40. She didn't listen to a thing and _____ all the objections.

    a. Manipulated
    b. Mired
    c. Furtive
    d. Rebuffed

ANSWER KEY

1. D
Femur NOUN A thighbone.

2. C
Metric System a system of measurements that is based on the base units of the meter/metre, the kilogram, the second, the ampere, the kelvin, the mole, and the candela.

3. D
Cousins NOUN the son or daughter of a person's uncle or aunt; a first cousin.

4. A
Helicopter

5. B
Schoolwork

6. D
Enthusiasm NOUN intensity of feeling; excited interest or eagerness.

7. C
Veterinarian NOUN medical doctor who treats non-human animals.

8. A
Immune ADJECTIVE protected by inoculation, or due to innate resistance to pathogens.

9. D
Pesticide NOUN a substance, usually synthetic although sometimes biological, used to kill or contain the activities of pests.

10. A
Famine NOUN a period of extreme shortage of food in a region.

11. B
Hormones NOUN any substance produced by one tissue

and conveyed by the bloodstream to another to effect physiological activity.

12. D
Foliage NOUN the leaves of plants.

13. A
Monsoons NOUN tropical rainy season when the rain lasts for several months with few interruptions.

14. B
Moss NOUN any of various small green plants growing on the ground or on the surfaces of trees, stones etc.

15. A
Extinguish NOUN to put out, as in fire; to end burning; to quench.

16. C
Convection NOUN the vertical movement of heat and moisture.

17. B
Ethanol NOUN a type of alcohol used as fuel.

18. A
Respiratory NOUN relating to respiration; breathing.

19. D
Reusable NOUN able to be used again; especially after salvaging or special treatment or processing.

20. B
Combustible NOUN capable of burning.

21. D
Conclusive ADJECTIVE providing an end to something; decisive.

22. D
Deftly ADVERB quickly and neatly in action.

23. C
Dupe VERB to swindle, deceive, or trick.

24. D
Designate ADJECTIVE appointed; chosen.

25. A
Dispel VERB to drive away by scattering, or so to cause to vanish; to clear away.

26. B
Frugal ADJECTIVE cheap, economical, thrifty.

27. B
Baubles NOUN a cheap showy ornament.

28. D
Creditors NOUN a person to whom a debt is owed.

29. A
Oratory NOUN the art of public speaking, especially in a formal, expressive, or forceful manner.

30. B
Liquidate VERB to convert assets into cash.

31. A
Hoax NOUN to deceive (someone) by making them believe something which has been maliciously or mischievously fabricated.

32. C
Deficient ADJECTIVE lacking something essential.

33. B
Grovel VERB to abase oneself before another person.

34. B
Intolerable ADJECTIVE not capable of being borne or endured; not proper or right to be allowed; insufferable; insupportable; unbearable.

35. A
Heirloom NOUN A valued possession that has been passed down through the generations.

36. B
Prevalent ADJECTIVE Widespread.

37. B
Nonchalant ADJECTIVE Casually calm and relaxed.

38. B
Pulverizes VERB to completely destroy, especially by crushing to fragments or a powder.

39. A
Stagnant ADJECTIVE lacking freshness, motion, flow, progress, or change; stale; motionless; still.

40. D
Rebuff NOUN a sudden resistance or refusal. [12]

Top 100 Common Vocabulary.

Learning vocabulary, especially in a hurry for an exam, means that you will be making friends with a lot of different word lists. Below is a word list of top 100 "must know" vocabulary to get you started.

When studying word lists, think of different ways to mix-it-up. Work with a friend or a study groups and compare word lists and test each other, or make flash cards.

1. **Abate** VERB reduce or lesson.
2. **Abandon** VERB to give up completely.
3. **Aberration** NOUN something unusual, different from the norm.
4. **Abet** VERB to encourage or support.
5. **Abstain** VERB to refrain from doing something.
6. **Abrogate** VERB to abolish or render void.
7. **Aesthetic** ADJECTIVE pertaining to beauty.
8. **Abstemious** ADJECTIVE moderate in the use of food or drink.
9. **Anachronistic** ADJECTIVE out of the context of time, out of date.
10. **Acrimonious** ADJECTIVE sharp or harsh in language or temper.
11. **Asylum** NOUN sanctuary, place of safety.
12. **Banal** ADJECTIVE lacking in freshness, originality, or vigor.
13. **Bias** NOUN a prejudice towards something or against something.
14. **Belie** VERB to give a false idea of.
15. **Brazen** ADJECTIVE bold.
16. **Belligerent** ADJECTIVE engaged in war.
17. **Camaraderie** NOUN togetherness, trust, group dynamic of trust.
18. **Cabal** NOUN a small group of persons engaged in plotting.
19. **Capacious** ADJECTIVE very large, spacious.
20. **Callous** ADJECTIVE unfeeling or insensitive.
21. **Clairvoyant** ADJECTIVE can predict the future.
22. **Cantankerous** ADJECTIVE ill-natured; quarrelsome.

23. **Compassion** NOUN sympathy.
24. **Captious** ADJECTIVE quick to find fault about trifle.
25. **Condescending** ADJECTIVE patronizing.
26. **Chauvinist** NOUN an extreme patriot.
27. **Conformist** NOUN someone who follows the majority.
28. **Clamorous** VERB loud and noisy.
29. **Deleterious** ADJECTIVE harmful.
30. **Deference** NOUN submitting to the wishes or judgment of another.
31. **Digression** NOUN straying from main point.
32. **Delectable** ADJECTIVE very pleasing.
33. **Discredit** NOUN dishonor someone, prove something untrue.
34. **Demeanor** NOUN behavior; bearing.
35. **Divergent** ADJECTIVE moving apart, going in different directions.
36. **Edict** NOUN a public command or proclamation issued by an authority.
37. **Emulate** NOUN following someone else's example.
38. **Effete** ADJECTIVE no longer productive; hence, lacking in or, worn out.
39. **Ephemeral** ADJECTIVE fleeting, temporary.
40. **Elicit** VERB to draw out.
41. **Exemplary** ADJECTIVE outstanding.
42. **Elucidate** VERB to make clear; to explain florid: ornate.
43. **Forbearance** NOUN patience, restraint.
44. **Facade** NOUN front or face, especially of a building.
45. **Fortuitous** ADJECTIVE lucky.
46. **Fallacious** ADJECTIVE unsound; misleading; deceptive.
47. **Fraught** NOUN filled with.
48. **Flaccid** ADJECTIVE lacking firmness.
49. **Ghastly** ADJECTIVE horrible, deathlike.
50. **Grimace** NOUN a distortion of the face to express an attitude or feeling.
51. **Hedonist** NOUN person who acts in pursuit of pleasure.
52. **Harbinger** NOUN a forerunner; ail announcer.
53. **Impetuous** ADJECTIVE rash, impulsive.
54. **Immaculate** ADJECTIVE spotless; pure.

55. **Inconsequential** ADJECTIVE without consequence, trivial, does not matter.
56. **Impeccable** ADJECTIVE faultless.
57. **Intrepid** ADJECTIVE fearless.
58. **Imprecation** NOUN a curse.
59. **Jubilation** NOUN extreme happiness, joy.
60. **Latent** ADJECTIVE hidden; present but not fully developed.
61. **Longevity** NOUN long (particularly long life).
62. **Maudlin** ADJECTIVE sentimental to the point of tears.
63. **Nonchalant** ADJECTIVE casual, calm, at ease.
64. **Oblivious** ADJECTIVE forgetful; absent-minded.
65. **Orator** NOUN speaker.
66. **Obviate** VERB to prevent, dispose of, or make un necessary by appropriate actions.
67. **Parched** ADJECTIVE lacking water, dried up.
68. **Panacea** NOUN a remedy for all ills.
69. **Pragmatic** ADJECTIVE practical.
70. **Paraphrase** VERB to restate the meaning of a passage in other words.
71. **Pretentious** ADJECTIVE being self important, thinking you are better than others.
72. **Pecuniary** ADJECTIVE pertaining to money.
73. **Prosaic** ADJECTIVE ordinary.
74. **Pensive** ADJECTIVE sadly thoughtful.
75. **Provocative** ADJECTIVE causes a fuss, inflammatory, likely to get people riled up.
76. **Peruse** VERB to read carefully.
77. **Querulous** ADJECTIVE irritable, prone to argument.
78. **Radical** NOUN one who advocates extreme basic changes.
79. **Reclusive** ADJECTIVE hermit, withdrawn.
80. **Recapitulate** VERB to restate in a brief, concise form.
81. **Renovate** VERB to make new, being redone.
82. **Refute** VERB to prove incorrect or false.
83. **Reverence** NOUN deep respect.
84. **Sallow** ADJECTIVE sick.
85. **Scrutinize** VERB to look at carefully.
86. **Sanguinary** ADJECTIVE bloody.
87. **Spurious** ADJECTIVE false, untrue.

88. **Scourge** VERB to punish severely; to afflict; to whip.
89. **Substantiate** VERB to confirm, prove.
90. **Scrutinize** VERB to examine carefully.
91. **Superficial** ADJECTIVE shallow.
92. **Sleazy** ADJECTIVE flimsy and cheap.
93. **Surreptitious** ADJECTIVE secret.
94. **Tactful** ADJECTIVE polite.
95. **Tangible** ADJECTIVE real; actual.
96. **Transient** ADJECTIVE temporary, impermanent.
97. **Vanquish** VERB to subdue or conquer.
98. **Vindicate** VERB to free from blame.
99. **Wary** ADJECTIVE careful, watchful.
100. **Zenith** NOUN the highest point.

Word List 2 – Stem Words

Probably the best way of learning new vocabulary is our "two-for-one" strategy of learning a stem word and then you can recognize two, three or more words that use the stem word. If you are studying for an exam with a vocabulary section, this is the best strategy for you.

Below is an extensive list of stem words with their meaning and examples. Following this list are 100 questions. These are divided into two question styles. In Part I, you are given the stem and asked to choose the meaning, and in Part II you are given the meaning and asked to choose the stem.

A

Root	Meaning	Examples
ab-, a-, abs-	away	abnormal, abrasion, absent, abstract, aversion
ac-, acu-	sharp, pointed	acupuncture
acr(i)-	sharp, pungent	acrid, acrimony
acr(o)-	height, summit	acrobatics, acromegaly, acronym, acrophobia,
ad-, a-, ac-, af-, ag-, al-, ap-, ar-, as-, at-	movement to or toward; in addition	adapt, affect, ascend, accept
aer-, aero-	air, atmosphere	aeronautics, aerosol
aesthet-	feeling, sensation	aesthetics, anaesthetic
agri-, egri	field, country	agriculture, peregrine
am-, amat-, amor-	love, loved,	amateur, amorous

A con't

Root	Meaning	Examples
ambi-	on both sides	ambidexterity, ambivalent
amic-, -imic-	friend	amicable, inimical
ant-, anti-	against, opposed to, preventive	antibiotic, antipodes
ante-, anti-	before, in front of, prior to	antebellum, antediluvian, anticipate, antiquarian
anthropo-	human	anthropology, anthropomorphic
aqu-	water	aquamarine, aquarium, aqueduct
arche-, archi-	ruler	archangel, archetype
archaeo-, archeo-	ancient	archaeology or archeology, archaic
arthr(o)-	joint	arthritis, arthropod
astr-, astro-	star, star-shaped	asterisk, astrology, astronomy, disaster
athl-	prize	athlete, pentathlon
aud(i)-	hearing, listening, sound	auditorium, auditory
aut-, auto-	self; directed from within	automobile, autonomy
avi-	bird	aviary, aviation

B

Root	Meaning	Examples
bac-	rod-shaped	bacilla, bacteria
baro-	weight, pressure	barometer, barograph,
basi-	at the bottom	basic, basis
bell(i)-	war	bellicose, belligerent
ben-	good, well	benefit, benignity
bi-	two	binoculars, bigamy, biscotti
bibl-	book	bibliography, bible
bi(o)-	life	biology, biologist, biosphere

B con't

Root	Meaning	Examples
brev(i)-	brief, short (time)	abbreviation, brevity
burs-, bursa	pouch, purse	bursar, bursary, disburse,

C

Root	Meaning	Examples
calc-	stone	calculus, calcite, calcium
can(i)-	dog	canine, Canis Major
cand-	glowing, iridescent	candid, incandescent, candle, candela
cap-, -cip-, capt-, -cept-	hold, take	capture, captive, conception, recipient
capit-, -cipit-	head	capital, decapitation, precipitation
capr-	goat	Capricorn, caprine
cardi(o)-	relating to the heart	cardiology, cardiograph
carp-	relating to the wrist	carpal, carpal tunnel syndrome
cata-	down	catastrophe, catabolic, cathode,
cav-	hollow	cave, cavity, excavation
ced-, cess-	go	procession, recede
celer-	quick	acceleration, celerity
cent-	hundred	cent, centennial, centurion
cervic-	relating to the neck, relating to the cervix	cervix, cervical
chloro-	green	chlorine, chlorophyll, chloroplast
choreo	dance	choreograph, choreography
chron-	time	chronic, chronometer, chronology
circum-	around	circumference, circumcise
clar-	clear	clarity, declaration
claud-, -clud-, claus-,-clus-	close	clause, exclusion,

How to Improve your Vocabulary 149

C con't

Root	Meaning	Examples
		include
clav-	key	conclave, clavicle
clement-	mild	clemency, inclement
clin-	bed, lean	recline declination, inclined
cogn-	know	cognitive, cognizant, recognize
con-, co-, col-, com-, cor-	with, together	connect, collide, compress
con(o)-	cone	conic, conical
contra-	against	contrast, contradict ("say against")
cord-	heart	accord, cordial
corn-	horn	cornea, cornucopia, unicorn, cornified
coron-	crown	corona, coronation
corpor-	body	corporation, corpse, corpuscle
cosmet(o)-		cosmetics, cosmetology
cre-	make	creation, creature
cred-	believe, trust	credibility, credentials
cris-, crit-	judge	crisis, critic
cruc(i)-	cross	crucial, crucifix, crucify, excruciating
crypt-	hidden	cryptic, cryptography
cub-	cube	cubic, cuboid
culp-	blame, fault	culpable, exculpate
cune-	wedge	cuneiform
curr-, curs-	run	concurrent, recursion, cursive, current
cycl(o)-	circular	bicycle, cycle, cyclone

D

Root	Meaning	Examples
damn-, -demn-	to inflict loss	condemn, damnation

D con't

Root	Meaning	Examples
de-	from, away from, removing	delete, demented
deca-, dec-, deka-, dek-	Ten	decagram, decahedron
decim-	tenth part	decimal, decimate
dem-, demo-	people	demagogue, democracy
dens-	thick	condense, density
dent-	tooth	dental, dentures
derm-	skin	dermis, epidermis, hypodermic
dia-	apart, through	dialysis, diameter
dict-	say, speak	contradict, dictation, dictionary, edict, predict
doc-, doct-	teach	docile, doctor
dogmat-, dox-	opinion, tenet	dogmatic, orthodox
dorm-	sleep	dormant, dormitory
duc-, duct-	lead	abduction, introduction, production, reduction, deduction
dur-	hard	durable, duration, duress, endure

E

Root	Meaning	Examples
eco-	house	ecology, economics,
ego-	self, I (first person)	egocentric
em-, empt-	buy	exemption, redeem
emul-	equal, rivaling	emulator
epi-, ep-	upon	epicenter, epoch
equ-, -iqu-	even, level	equal, equivalence
equ-	horse	Equestrian
erg-	work	ergonomics
err-	stray	aberration, errant
ethn	native	ethnicity, ethnic

E con't

Root	Meaning	Examples
eu-	well, good	euphoria, euthanasia
ex-, e-, ef-	from, out	exclude, extrude, extend
exo-	outside	exothermic
exter-, extra-	outer	exterior, extrasensory
extrem-	utmost, outermost	extremity, extremophile

F

Root	Meaning	Examples
f-, fat-	say, speak	fate, infant, preface
fac-, -fic-, fact, -fect-	make	defect, factory, manufacture
femin-	female	femininity, feminist
fall-, -fell-, fals	deceive	falsity, infallibility
fatu-	foolish, useless	fatuous, infatuation
feder-	treaty, agreement, contract, league	confederation, federal
fel-	cat	feline
felic-	happy, merry	felicity
fend-, fens-	prevent	defend, offense
fer-	carry	reference, transfer
fid-, fis-	faith, trust	confidence, fidelity
fin-	end	finish, final
find-, fiss-	split	fission, fissures
firm-	fix, settle	confirmation, firmament
fl-	blow	flatulence, inflation
flect-, flex-	bend	flexor, inflection
flig-, flict-	strike	conflict, inflict
flor-	flower	floral, florid
flu-, flux-	flow	effluent, fluency
form-	shape	conformity, deformity, formation
frang-, -fring-, fract-, frag-	break	fracture, fragment, frangible, infringe
frater-, fratr-	brother	fraternity
fric-, frict-	rub	dentifrice, friction

F con't

Root	Meaning	Examples
front-	forehead	confront, frontal
fug-, fugit-	flee refuge	centrifuge, fugitive,
fum-	smoke	fume, fumigation
fund-	bottom	fundamentalism, profundity
fund-, fus-	pour	effusion, profusion
fung-, funct-	do	function, fungibility

G

Root	Meaning	Examples
gastr-	stomach	gastric, gastroenterologist
germin-	sprout	germination
ger-, gest-	bear, carry	digest, gestation
glac-	slow, ice	glacier, glacial
glob-	sphere	global, globule
grad-, -gred-, gress-	walk, step,	grade, regress
gran-	grain	granary, granule
graph-	draw, write	graphic, graphology
greg-	flock	gregarious, segregation
gubern-	govern, pilot	gubernatorial
gymn-	nude	gymnasium, gymnosperm

H

Root	Meaning	Examples
hab-, -hib-, habit-, -hibit-	have	habit, prohibition
haem-	blood	haemophilia, hemoglobin
heli(o)-	sun	heliotrope, helium
hemi-	half	hemicycle, hemisphere
her-, hes-	cling	adhesive, coherent
herb-	grass	herbicide
hod-	way	cathode, hodometer,
hom(o)-	same	homosexual, homogenous
hor-	boundary	aphorism, horizon
hort(i)-	garden	horticulture, horticulturist
hospit-	host	hospitality, hospitable
hum-	ground	exhumation, inhume
hydr(o)-	water	hydrology, hydrophobia,

H con't

Root	Meaning	Examples
hydr(o)-		hydroponic, hydraulic, hydrlysis, hydrous, hydrophilic
hygr-	wet	hygrometer

I

Root	Meaning	Examples
idi(o)-	personal	idiom, idiosyncrasy, idiot
ign-	fire	igneous, ignition
in- (1), im-	in, on	incur, intend, invite
in- (2), il-, im-, ir-	not un- (negation)	illicit, impossible, irrational
infra-	below, under	infrastructure, infrared
insul-	island	insular, insulation
inter-	among, between	intercollegiate, intermission, intersection
irasc-, irat-	be angry	irascible, irate
is-, iso-	equal, the same	isometric, isomorphic, isotropic

J

Root	Meaning	Examples
jac- -ject-	cast, throw	eject, interject, ejaculate, trajectory
joc-	joke	jocularity
jug-	yoke	conjugal, subjugate
jung-, junct-	join	conjunction, juncture
janu-	door	janitor
jus-, jur-, judic-	law, justice	justice, jury, judge
juven-	young, youth	juvenile, rejuvenate
juxta-	beside, near	juxtaposition

K

Root	Meaning	Examples
kil(o)-	thousand	kilobyte, kilogram, kilometer
kine-	movement, motion	telekinesis, kinetic kinesthetic
klept-	steal	kleptomania
kudo-	glory	kudos

L

Root	Meaning	Examples
lab-, laps-	slide, slip	elapse, relapse
labi-	lip	bilabial, labial
labor-	toil	collaboration, elaboration
lacer-	tear	laceration, lacerate
lact-	milk	lactate, lactation, lactose
lamin-	layer, slice	laminate, lamination
larg-	large	enlargement, largess
larv-	ghost, mask	larva, larvae, larval
lax-	not tense	laxative, relaxation
leg-	law	legal, legislative
leon-	lion	Leo, leonine, Leopold
-less	lack of	penniless
lev-	lift, light	elevator, levitation
liber-	free	liberation, liberty
lig-	bind	ligament, ligature
lin-	line	linearity, line
lingu-	language, tongue	bilingual, linguistic
liter-	letter	alliteration, illiterate,
lith(o)-	stone	lithosphere, megalith, monolith, Neolithic Era
loc-	place	local, location
long-	long	elongate, longitude
loqu-, locut-	speak	allocution, eloquence
luc-	bright, light	Lucifer (bearer of light)
lud-, lus-	play	allude, illusion
lumin-	light	illumination, luminous
lun-	moon	lunar, lunatic
lysis	dissolving	analysis, cytolysis, hydrolysis

M

Root	Meaning	Examples
magn-	great, large	magnanimous, magnificent
maj-	greater	majesty, majority, majuscule
mal-	bad, wretched	malfeasance, malicious, malignancy
mamm-	breast	mammal, mammary gland
man-	stay	immanence

M con't

Root	Meaning	Examples
mand-	hand	mandate, remand
mania	mental illness	kleptomania, maniac
manu-	hand	manual, manuscript
mar-	sea	marine, maritime
mater-, matr-	mother	matriarch, matrix
maxim-	greatest	maximal, maximum
medi-, -midi-	middle	median, medieval
men(o)-	moon	menopause, menstruation
ment-	mind	demented, mentality
merc-	reward, wages	mercantile, merchant
merg-, mers-	dip, plunge	emerge, immersion
mes-	middle	mesolithic, mesozoic
meter-, metr-	measure	metric, thermometer
meta-	above, among, beyond	metaphor, metaphysical
micr(o)-	small	microphone, microscope
migr-	wander	emigrant, migrate
milit-	soldier	military, militia
mill-	thousand	millennium, million
mim-	repeat	mime, mimic
min-	less, smaller	minority, minuscule
mir-	wonder, amazement	admire, miracle, mirror
mis-	hate	misandry, misogyny
misce-, mixt-	mix	miscellaneous, mixture
mitt-, miss-	send	intermittent, missionary, transmission
mne-	memory	mnemonic
moll-	soft	emollient, mollify
mon(o)-	one	monolith, monotone
mont-	mountain	Montana
morph-	form, shape	anthropomorphism, morpheme, morphology
mort-	death	immortal, mortality, mortuary
mov-, mot-	move	motion mobile, momentum, motor, move
mulg-, muls-	milk	emulsion
mult(i)-	many, much	multiple, multiplex, multitude
mur-	wall	immured, mural
myth(o)-	story	mythic, mythology

N

Root	Meaning	Examples
narc-	numb	narcosis, narcotic
nas-	nose	nasal
nav-	ship	naval, navigate
neur-	nerve	neurology, neurosurgeon
nod-	knot	node, nodule
nov-	new	innovation, nova
nud-	naked	denude, nudity
nutri	nourish	nutrition, nutrient

O

Root	Meaning	Examples
ob-, o-, oc-, os-	against	obstinate, ostentatious, obstreperous
oct-	eight	octagon, octahedron
oct-	eight	octangular, octennial, octovir
octav-	eighth	octaval, octave
ocul-	eye	ocular, oculus
odor	smell	odorous, malodorous
omni-	all	omnipotence, omnivore
ophthalm-	eye	ophthalmology
opt-	eye	optical, optician
opt-	choose	adopt, optional
optim-	best	optimum
or-	mouth	oral, orator
ordin-	order	ordinal, ordinary
orn-	decorate	adorn, ornament, ornate
orth(o)-	straight	orthodoxy, orthosis
osteo-	bone	osteoporosis
ov-	egg	oval, ovule

P

Root	Meaning	Examples
pac-	peace	pacifism, pacifist
paed-, ped	child	paediatric, paedictrician
pagin-	page	pagination, paginate
pal-	stake	impalement, pale
pall-	be pale	pallid, pallor
pand-, pans-	spread	expand, expansion
par(a)-	beside, near	parallel, parameter
part(i)-	part	bipartite, partition

P con't

Root	Meaning	Examples
parthen(o)-	maiden	parthenogenesis
pasc-, past-	feed	pasture, repast
path-	feel, hurt	pathetic, pathology
pati-, pass-	suffer, feel, endure, permit	passive, patience
ped-	foot, child	pedal, quadruped, pediatric
pell-, puls-	drive	propellent, propulsor, repellent
pen-	almost	peninsula, penultimate, penumbra
pent-	five	pentagon
pept-	to digest	peptic, peptide
per-	thoroughly, through	perfection, persistence
peri-	around	perimeter, periscope
pet-	strive towards	appetite, competition
pharmac-	drug, medicine	pharmacy, pharmacist
phob-	fear	hydrophobia agoraphobia
phon(o)-	sound	homophone, microphone, phonograph
phos-, phot-	light	phosphor, photograph
plac-, -plic-	please	placebo, placid
plan-	flat	explanation, planar, plane
plas-	mould	plasma, plastic
plaud-, -plod-, plaus-, -plos-	clap	applaud, applause, explosion, implode
ple-, plet-	fill	complement, suppletion
plic-	fold	duplication, replicate
plum-	feather	plumage, plumate
pod-	foot	podiatry, tripod
pol-	pole	dipole, polar
pole-, poli-	city	metropolis, politics
pon-, posit-	put	component, position, postpone
ponder-	weight	preponderance
port-	carry	export, transportation
post-	after, behind	posterior, postscript
potam-	river	Mesopotamia, hippopotamus

P con't

Root	Meaning	Examples
pre-	before	prehistoric, previous
prim-	first	primary, primeval, primitive
prior-	former	priority
priv(i)-	separate	deprivation, privilege
proxim-	nearest	approximate, proximity
pubi-	sexually mature	pubescent, pubic
pugn-	fight	pugnacious, repugnant
pung-, punct-	prick	puncture, pungent
pup-	doll	pupa, puppet

Q

Root	Meaning	Examples
quadr-	four	quadrangle, quadrillion
quart-	fourth	quartary, quartile
quatern-	four each	quaternary, quaternion
quer-, -quir-, quesit-, -quisit-	search, seek	inquisition, query
quint-	fifth	quintary, quintile
quot-	how many, how great	quota, quotient

R

Root	Meaning	Examples
rad-, ras-	scrape, shave	abrade, abrasion
radi-	beam, spoke	radiance, radiation
ram-	branch	ramification, ramose
ranc-	rancidness, grudge, bitterness	rancid, rancor
rauc-	harsh, hoarse	raucous
re-, red-	again, back	recede, redact
reg-, -rig-, rect-	straight	dirigible, erect, erection, rectum
ren-	kidney	renal
rep-, rept-	crawl, creep	reptile

R con't

Root	Meaning	Examples
retro-	backward, behind	retrograde, retrospective, retrovirus
rid-, ris-	laugh	derision, ridicule
rod-, ros-	gnaw	corrode, erosion, rodent
ruber-, rubr-	red	rubric, ruby
rump-, rupt-	break	eruption, rupture

S

Root	Meaning	Examples
racchar-	sugar	saccharin
sacr-, secr-	sacred	consecrate, sacrament
sagitt-	arrow	sagittal plane, Sagittaria
sal-	salt	salinity
sali-, -sili-, salt-	jump	resilient, salient,
san-	healthy	insane, sanity
sanc-	holy	sanctify, sanctuary
sanguin-	blood	consanguinity, sanguine
sapi-, -sipi-	taste, wise	incipience, sapient
saur-	lizard, reptile	dinosaur
scab-	scratch	scabies
scal-	ladder, stairs	scalar, scale
scand-, -scend-, scans-, -scens-	climb	ascend, transcendent
sci-	know	prescient, science
scind-, sciss-	split	rescind, scissors
scop-, scept-	look at, examine, view, observe	horoscope, kaleidoscope, stethoscope
scrib-, script-	write	inscribe, scripture
se-, sed-	apart	secede, sedition
sec-, sect-, seg-	cut	section, segment
sed-	settle, calm	sedative, sedate
sed-, -sid-, sess-	sit	reside, sediment, session, supersede
sema-	sign	semantics, semaphore
sen-	old man	senator, senility
senti-, sens-	feel	consensus, sentient

S con't

Root	Meaning	Examples
sequ-, secut-	follow	consecutive, sequence
serp-	crawl, creep	serpent
serv-	save, protect	conservation
set-	bristle, hair	seta, setose
sever-	stern, strict, serious	severity
sign-	sign	design, designate, signal
sil-	quiet or still	silence
silv(i)-	forest	silviculture
simi-	ape, monkey	simian
simil-	likeness, trust, group	assimilate, similarity
simul-	imitating, feigning	simulation
singul-	one each	singular
sinu-	(to draw) a line	insinuate
siph(o)-	tube	siphon
sist-	cause to stand	consist, persistence
soci-	group	associate, social
sol-	sun	solar
sol-	comfort	soothe, consolation
sol-	alone, only	desolate, sole, solo, solipsism
solv-, solut-	loosen, set free	dissolve, solution
soma-	body	somatic
somn-	sleep	insomnia
son-	sound	resonance
soph-	wise	sophist
sorb-, sorpt-	suck	absorb, absorption
sord-	dirt	sordid
soror-	sister	sorority
spati-	space	spatial
spec-, -spic-, spect-	look	conspicuous, inspection, specimen
spect-	watch, look at	spectator
specul-	observe	speculation

S con't

Root	Meaning	Examples
sper-	hope	desperation, esperance
spher-	ball	sphere, spheroid
spir-	breathe	respiration
squal-	scaly, dirty, filthy	squalid, squalor
st-	stand	stable, station, status, statistic, statue
stagn-	pool of standing water	stagnant
statu-, -stitu-	stand	institution, statute
stell-	star	constellation, stellar
still-	drip	distillation
stimul-	goad, rouse, excite	stimulate
stingu-, stinct-	apart	distinction, distinguish
string-, strict-	upright, stiff	stringent
stru-, struct-	structure, building	construction, construe
stud-	dedication	student
stup-	wonder	stupor
styl-	column, pillar	stylus
su-, sut-	sew	suture
sui-	self	suicide
suad-, suas-	urge	persuasion
suav-	sweet	suave
sub-, su-, sus-	below	submerge
subter-	under	subterfuge, subterranean
sum-, sumpt-	take	assumption, consume
supra-	above, over	supranationalism
syn-, sy-, syl-, sym-	with	symbol, symmetry, synonym, system

T

Root	Meaning	Examples
tac-, -tic-	be silent	reticent, tacit

T con't

Root	Meaning	Examples
tach-	swift	tachometer
tang-, -ting-, tact-, tag-	touch	contact, tactile, tangent
tard-	slow	retard
techn-	art, skill	technology
teg-, tect-	cover	integument, protection
tele-	far, end	telegram, telephone, telescope
tempor-	time	contemporary, temporal, temporary
ten-, -tin-, tent-	hold	continent, detention, tenacious, tenor
tend-, tens-	stretch	extend, extension
tenu-	slender, thin	attenuate, tenuous
ter-, trit-	rub	attrition, contrite
termin-	boundary, limit, end	determine, terminal, termination
terr-	dry land	terrace, terracotta, terrain
terti-	third	tertian, tertiary
test-	witness	testament, testimony
tetr-	four	tetrahedron
tex-, text-	weave	texture, textile
than-	death	euthanasia
the-	put	theme, thesis
the(o)-, thus-	god	theology, enthusiasm
therm-	heat, warm	thermometer, endotherm
tim-	be afraid	timid
ting-, tinct-	moisten	tincture
ton-	stretch	tone, isotonic
top-	place	topic, topography
torqu-, tort-	twist	extortion, torque, torture
tot-	all, whole	total, totality
trans-, tra-, tran-	across	tradition, transcend, transportation
trapez-	four-sided, table	trapezoid trapezius
traum-	wound	trauma, traumatic
tri-	three	triad, tripod

T con't

Root	Meaning	Examples
tri-	three	triangle, trivia, triumvirate
trud-, trus-	thrust	extrusion, intrude
typ-	stamp, model	archetype, phenotype, typography

U

Root	Meaning	Examples
ultim-	farthest	ultimatum, ultimate
umbilic	navel	umbilical
umbr-	shade, shadow	penumbra, umbrella
un-, uni-	one	unary, union
und-	wave	abundant, undulate
urb-	city	urban
ut-, us-	use	usual, utility

V

Root	Meaning	Examples
vac-	empty	vacancy, vacation, vacuum
vad-, vas-	go	evade, pervasive
vag-	wander	vague, vagabond
vap-	lack (of)	evaporation, vapid, vaporize
veh-, vect-	carry	vehicle, vector
vel-	veil	revelation, velate
ven-, vent-	come	advent, convention
vend-	sell	vendor, vending
vener-	respectful	veneration, venereal
vent-	wind	ventilation
ver-	true	verify, verity
verb-	word	verbal, verbatim, verbosity
verber-	whip	reverberation
vert-, vers-	turn	convert, inversion, invert, vertical
vest-	clothe, garment	divest, vest
vestig-	follow, track	investigate
veter-	old	inveterate, veteran
vi-	way	deviate, obvious, via
vic-	change	vice versa, vicissitude
vid-, vis-	see	video, vision
vil-	cheap	vile, vilify

V con't

Root	Meaning	Examples
vinc-, vict-	conquer	invincible, victory
viti-	fault	vice, vitiate
viv-	live	revive, survive, vivid
voc-	voice	vocal, vocation, provocative
volv-, volut-	roll	convolution, revolve
vor-, vorac-	swallow	devour, voracious
vulg-	common, crowd	divulge, vulgarity, vulgate

X

Root	Meaning	Examples
xen-	foreign	xenophobia

Z

Root	Meaning	Examples
zo-	animal, living being	protozoa, zoo, zoology
zon-	belt, girdle	zone
zym-	ferment	enzyme, lysozyme [11]

Stem Words Practice Questions
Part I.

1. Choose the meaning of the stem word agri-

    a. Markings

    a. Development

    a. Field

    a. Government

2. Choose the meaning of the stem word ambi-

    a. Health study

    b. Cellular tissue

    c. Stretched out

    d. On both sides

3. Choose the meaning of the stem word baro-

    a. Weight or pressure

    b. North

    c. Brief

    d. Greatness

4. Choose the meaning of the stem word bibl-

    a. At the bottom

    b. Deep

    c. Book

    d. Wood

5. Choose the meaning of the stem word calc-

    a. Pretty

    b. Stone

    c. Weak

    d. Vault

6. Choose the meaning of the stem word cand-

    a. Long

    b. Goat like

    c. Harden

    d. Glowing

7. Choose the meaning of the stem word damn-

    a. To inflict loss upon

    b. Tenth part

    c. Leadership

    d. Move away from

8. Choose the meaning of the stem word derm-

    a. Above

    b. Skin

    c. Insane actions

    d. Fingers

9. Choose the meaning of the stem word emul-

    a. View

    b. In support

    c. Striving to equal

    d. Against

10. Choose the meaning of the stem word fatu-

   a. Shape
   b. Foolish or useless
   c. Wind direction
   d. Size

11. Choose the meaning of the stem word equ-

   a. Even or level
   b. Knowledge
   c. Inside or within
   d. House

12. Choose the meaning of the stem word fel-

   a. Opportunity
   b. Widow
   c. Female
   d. Cat

13. Choose the meaning of the stem word gastr-

   a. Stomach
   b. Formality
   c. Appearance
   d. Related to health

14. Choose the meaning of the stem word germin-

   a. Small animals
   b. Race
   c. Sprout
   d. Ice

15. Choose the meaning of the stem word haem-

a. Mental state
b. Blood
c. Child health
d. Time

16. Choose the meaning of the stem word hemi-

a. Half
b. Air
c. Strange
d. Foreign

17. Choose the meaning of the stem word infra-

a. Doubtful
b. Foundation
c. Strength
d. Below or under

18. Choose the meaning of the stem word insul-

a. Angry state
b. Puncturing
c. Island
d. Again

19. Choose the meaning of the stem word janu-

a. Law
b. Yoke
c. Door
d. Direction

20. Choose the meaning of the stem word junct-

   a. Sound
   b. Join
   c. Jungle
   d. Electricity

21. Choose the meaning of the stem word klept-

   a. General
   b. Shy person
   c. Lawful
   d. Steal

22. Choose the meaning of the stem word -less

   a. Fast in movement
   b. Lack of
   c. Related to dressing or grooming
   d. Advantage over

23. Choose the meaning of the stem word kudo-

   a. Force
   b. Thousand
   c. Glory
   d. Inflammation

24. Choose the meaning of the stem word labi-

   a. Lips
   b. Layers
   c. Delay
   d. Secure

25. Choose the meaning of the stem word lact-

a. Shine

b. Milk

c. Lecture

d. Teaching

26. Choose the meaning of the stem word lingu-

a. Teacher

b. Language, tongue

c. Knowledge

d. Tribes

27. Choose the meaning of the stem word magn-

a. Hand

b. Breast

c. Small in size

d. Great, large

28. Choose the meaning of the stem word mamm-

a. Breast

b. Bad

c. Stay

d. Long

29. Choose the meaning of the stem word nas-

a. Large ship

b. Death

c. Foot

d. Nose

30. Choose the meaning of the stem word nav-

   a. Slime

   b. Ship

   c. Join

   d. Tell

31. Choose the meaning of the stem word octav-

   a. Fearless

   b. Against

   c. Eye

   d. Eighth

32. Choose the meaning of the stem word odor-

   a. Fragrance

   b. Creepy

   c. Sad

   d. Shady

33. Choose the meaning of the stem word optim-

   a. Order

   b. Best

   c. Swing

   d. Straight

34. Choose the meaning of the stem word pac-

   a. Feed

   b. Ancient

   c. Peace

   d. Maiden

35. Choose the meaning of the stem word patr-

   a. Endure

   b. Father

   c. Few

   d. Money

36. Choose the meaning of the stem word pent-

   a. Five

   b. Control

   c. Around

   d. Properly

37. Choose the meaning of the stem word pup-

   a. Four

   b. Doll

   c. Punish

   d. Wolf

38. Choose the meaning of the stem word quart-

   a. Fourth

   b. Quiet

   c. Rest

   d. Milk

39. Choose the meaning of the stem word rauc-

   a. Crawl or creep

   b. Root

   c. Harsh or hoarse

   d. Originate

40. Choose the meaning of the stem word rept-

   a. Mental illness
   b. Creep or crawl
   c. Repetition
   d. Timely

41. Choose the meaning of the stem word retro-

   a. Backward or behind
   b. Air less
   c. Kidney
   d. Nose or snout

42. Choose the meaning of the stem word rupt-

   a. Gnaw
   b. Prow
   c. Throat
   d. Break

43. Choose the meaning of the stem word sal-

   a. Anger
   b. Salt
   c. Jump
   d. Save

44. Choose the meaning of the stem word sacr-

   a. Sacred
   b. Flesh
   c. Scratch
   d. Seriousness

45. Choose the meaning of the stem word saur-

   a. Surround

   a. Fish

   a. Reptile or lizard

   a. Ladder

46. Choose the meaning of the stem word tard-

   a. Slow

   b. Shy

   c. Touch

   d. Hard

47. Choose the meaning of the stem word techn-

   a. Improvement

   b. Shocking

   c. Art, skill

   d. Complete

48. Choose the meaning of the stem word termin-

   a. God

   b. Machine

   c. Boundary or end

   d. Weave

49. Choose the meaning of the stem word therm-

   a. Heat or warm

   b. Beast

   c. Ice

   d. Regulator

50. Choose the meaning of the stem word ultim-
   a. Fruitful
   b. Farthest
   c. Infection
   d. Shadow

Answer Key

1. C
The stem word agri- means relating to field, for example agriculture.

2. D
The stem word ambi- means on both sides, for example ambivalent.

3. A
The stem word baro- means relating to weight or pressure, for example barometer.

4. C
The stem word bibl- relates to books, for example bibliography and bible.

5. B The stem word calc- means stone, for example calcium.

6. D
The stem word cand- means glowing, for examples candle and candid.

7. A
The stem word damn- means to inflict loss upon, for example condemn and damnation.

8. B
The stem word derm- relates to skin, for example dermis and epidermis.

9. C
The stem word emul- means striving to equal, for example emulation.

10. B
The stem word fatu- means foolish or useless, for example fatuous and infatuation.

11. A
The stem word equ- means even or level, for example equal.

12. D
The stem word fel- means relating to cat, for example feline.

13. A
The stem word gastr- means leading, for example gastric.

14. C
The stem word germin- means sprout, for example germination.

15. B
The stem word haem- means blood, for example hemophilia.

16. A
The stem word hemi- means half, for example hemisphere.

17. D
The stem word infra- means below and under, for example infrastructure.

18. C
The stem word insul- means island, for example insulate.

19. C
The stem word janu- means door, for example janitor.

20. B
The stem word junct- means join, for example junction.

21. D
The stem word klept- means steal, for example kleptomaniac.

22. B
The stem word -less means lack of, for example useless and homeless.

23. C
The stem word kudo- means glory, for example kudos.

24. A
The stem word labi- means lips, for example labial.

25. B
The stem word lact- means milk, for example lactate.

26. B
The stem word lingu- means relating to language, tongue, for example bilingual and linguistic.

27. D
The stem word magn- means great, large, for example magnanimous and magnificent.

28. A
The stem word mamm- means breast, for example mammal.

29. D
The stem word nas- means nose, for example nasal.

30. B
The stem word nav- means ship, for example naval.

31. D
The stem word octav- means eighth, for examples octaval.

32. A
The stem word odor- means fragrance, for example odorous.

33. B
The stem word optim- means best, for example optimum and optimal.

34. C
The stem word pac- means peace, for example pact and pacify.

35. B
The stem word patr- means father, for example patriarch.

36. A
The stem word pent- means five, for example pentagon.

37. B
The stem word pup- means doll, for example puppet.

38. A
The stem word quart- means fourth, for example quartile.

39. C
The stem word rauc- means harsh or hoarse, for example raucous.

40. B
The stem word rept- means to crawl or creep, for example reptile.

41. A
The stem word retro- means backward or behind, for example retrospect and retrograde.

42. D
The stem word rupt- means break, for example rupture.

43. B
The stem word sal- means salt, for example salinity or saline.

44. A
The stem word sacr- means sacred, for example consecrate and sacrament.

45. C
The stem word saur- means reptile or lizard, for example dinosaur.

46. A
The stem word tard- means slow, for example retard or tardy.

47. C
The stem word techn- means art, skill, for example technician.

48. C
The stem word termin- means boundary or end, for examples termination and terminal.

49. A

The stem word therm- means heat or warm, for example thermal and thermostat.

50. B

The stem word ultim- means farthest, for example ultimate.[11]

Stem Words Practice Part II.

1. Choose the stem word that means air or atmosphere.

    a. Bran-

    b. Gen-

    c. Aero-

    d. Agog-

2. Choose the stem word that means love, loved.

    a. Amor-

    b. Cand-

    c. Glan-

    d. Mania-

3. Choose the stem word that means women, female.

    a. Fam-

    b. Ward-

    c. Gust-

    d. Femin-

4. Choose the stem word that means end.

    a. Gran-

    b. Fin-

    c. Flux-

    d. Eur-

5. Choose the stem word that means life.

    a. Bio-

    b. Calcu-

    c. Ext-

    d. Ago-

6. Choose the stem word that means outermost, utmost.

    a. Frug-

    b. Etym-

    c. Larg-

    d. Extrem-

7. Choose the stem word that means at the bottom.

    a. Trid-

    b. Eco-

    c. Basi-

    d. Ful-

8. Choose the stem word that means relating to the heart.

    a. Cardio-

    b. Hea-

    c. Dimu-

    d. Gel-

9. Choose the stem word that means relating to dance.

    a. Dan-

    b. Fund-

    c. Choreo-

    d. Andr-

10. Choose the stem word that means finger, toe, digit.

    a. Horti-

    b. Dactyl-

    c. Calcu-

    d. Drim-

11. Choose the stem word that means tenth part.

   a. Decim-
   b. Tenr-
   c. Frug-
   d. Hect-

12. Choose the stem word that means self, I (first person).

   a. Ere-
   b. Ego-
   c. Selfi-
   d. Manu-

13. Choose the stem word that means ice.

   a. Tor-
   b. Janu-
   c. Cool-
   d. Glaci-

14. Choose the stem word that means host.

   a. Hospit-
   b. Habi-
   c. Proc-
   d. Paci-

15. Choose the stem word that means grass.

   a. Frau-
   b. Lea-
   c. Herb-
   d. Le-

16. Choose the stem word that means people, race, tribe, nation.

    a. Adul-

    b. Baro-

    c. Cad-

    d. Ethn-

17. Choose the stem word that means idea; thought.

    a. Cupl(u)-

    b. Stat-

    c. Ide(o)-

    d. Anal-

18. Choose the stem word that means among, between.

    a. Chang-

    b. Sta-

    c. Inter-

    d. Less-

19. Choose the stem word that means young, youth.

    a. Juven-

    b. Yot-

    c. Drap-

    d. Rabi-

20. Choose the stem word that means not tense.

    a. Hommi-

    b. Lax-

    c. -Tic

    d. Tens-

21. Choose the stem word that means mental illness.
   a. Kilm-
   b. Cher-
   c. Mania-
   d. Logy-

22. Choose the stem word that means greater.
   a. Cede-
   b. Culp-
   c. Maj-
   d. Lar-

23. Choose the stem word that means light.
   a. Lumin-
   b. Radi-
   c. Scope-
   d. Promu-

24. Choose the stem word that means nourish.
   a. Phon-
   b. Feast-
   c. Nal-
   d. Nutri-

25. Choose the stem word that means eight.
   a. Kine-
   b. Zeb-
   c. Oct-
   d. Puin-

26. Choose the stem word that means movement, motion.

    a. Kis-

    b. Kine-

    c. Trid-

    d. Agog-

27. Choose the stem word that means child.

    a. Dropi-

    b. Calp-

    c. Ped-

    d. Small-

28. Choose the stem word that means fifth.

    a. Quint-

    b. Ward-

    c. Caldi-

    d. Scor-

29. Choose the stem word that means kidney.

    a. Crop-

    b. Tic-

    c. Mia-

    d. Ren-

30. Choose the stem word that means scratch.

    a. Pus-

    b. Scab-

    c. Hetro-

    d. -Agog

31. Choose the stem word that means three.

a. Hank-

b. Qua-

c. Tri-

d. Quart-

32. Choose the stem word that means navel.

a. Umbilic-

b. Hyal-

c. Infra-

d. Ful-

33. Choose the stem word that means city.

a. Macro-

b. Larv-

c. Jac-

d. Urb-

34. Choose the stem word that means empty.

a. Odor-

b. Vac-

c. Mar-

d. Nema-

35. Choose the stem word that means respectful.

a. Ocul-

b. Nunci-

c. Vener-

d. Pecum-

36. Choose the stem word that means foreign.

   a. Xen-

   b. Fora-

   c. Crati-

   d. Lanu-

37. Choose the stem word that means animal, living being.

   a. Ery-

   b. Brat(o)-

   c. Anis-

   d. Zo-

38. Choose the stem word that means save, protect, and serve.

   a. Tor-

   b. Ony-

   c. Serv-

   d. Pall-

39. Choose the stem word that means before.

   a. Hered-

   b. Pre-

   c. Part-

   d. Jug-

40. Choose the stem word that means bone.

   a. Osteo-

   b. Hirsut-

   c. Onym-

   d. Scien-

41. Choose the stem word that means tear.

    a. Lacer-

    b. Hod-

    c. Lapid-

    d. Mand-

42. Choose the stem word that means be angry.

    a. Calcu-

    b. Irat-

    c. Ped-

    d. Gram-

43. Choose the stem word that means end.

    a. Grou-

    b. Stari-

    c. Fin-

    d. Ladi-

44. Choose the stem word that means outside.

    a. Exo-

    b. Deca-

    c. Derac-

    d. Huri-

45. Choose the stem word that means word.

    a. Nauti-

    b. Baro-

    c. Justi-

    d. Verb-

46. Choose the stem word that means sphere.

   a. Curv-
   b. Glob-
   c. Blob-
   d. Derog-

47. Choose the stem word that means prize.

   a. Athl-
   b. Grad-
   c. Baco-
   d. Infi-

48. Choose the stem word that means hollow.

   a. Infor-
   b. Bio-
   c. Cav-
   d. Logy-

49. Choose the stem word that means wet.

   a. Hygr-
   b. Justi-
   c. Quac-
   d. Hedron-

50. Choose the stem word that means joke.

   a. Funi-
   b. Archy-
   c. Ward-
   d. Joc-

STEM WORD ANSWER KEY PART II.

1. C

The stem root word aero- means air, atmosphere, for example, aeronautics and aerosol.

2. A

The stem root word amor- means love, loved, for example amorous.

3. D

The stem root word femin- means relating to women, female, for example femininity.

4. B

The stem root word fin-means end, for example finish and final.

5. A

The stem root word bi(o)- means life, for example, biology, biologist and biosphere.

6. D

The stem root word extrem- means outermost, utmost, for example extremity.

7. C

The stem root word basi- means at the bottom, for example basic and basis.

8. A

The stem root word cardi(o)- means heart, for example cardiology, cardiograph.

9. C

The stem root word choreo- means dance, for example choreography.

10. B

The stem root word dactyl- means finger, toe, digit, word, for example pterodactyl.

11. A
The stem root word decim- means relating to tenth part, for example decimal and decimate.

12. B
The stem root word ego- means relating to self, I (first person), for example egocentric.

13. D
The stem root word glaci- means relating to ice, for example glacier.

14. A
The stem root word hospit- means host, for example hospitality.

15. C
The stem root word herb- means grass, for example, herbicide.

16. D
The stem root word ethn- means people, race, tribe, nation, for example ethnic and ethnicity.

17. C
The stem root word ide(o)- means power, for example ideogram and ideology.

18. C
The stem root word inter- means among or between, for example intercollegiate, intermission and intersection.

19. A
The stem root word juven- means young or youth, for example juvenile, rejuvenate.

20. B
The stem root word lax- means not tense, for example laxative and relaxation.

21. C
The stem root word mania- means relating to mental illness, for example kleptomania and maniac.

22. C
The stem root word maj- means greater, for example majesty, majority.

23. A
The stem root word lumin- means light, for example illumination and luminous.

24. D
The stem root word nutri- means nourish, for example nutrient.

25. C
The stem root word oct- means eight, for example octagon and octahedron.

26. B
The stem root word kine- means air movement, motion, for example telekinesis, kinetic energy and kinesthetic.

27. C
The stem root word ped- means child, for example pedagogy.

28. A
The stem root word quint- means fifth, for example quinary and quintet.

29. D
The stem root word ren- means kidney, for example renal.

30. B
The stem root word scab- means scratch for example scabies.

31. C
The stem root word tri- means three for example triad and tripod.

32. A
The stem root word umbilic- means navel, for example umbilical.

33. D
The stem root word urb- means city, for example urban.

34. B
The stem root word vac- means empty, for example vacancy, vacation and vacuum.

35. C
The stem root word vener- means respectful, word, for example veneration and venereal.

36. A
The stem root word xen- means foreign, for example xenophobia.

37. D
The stem root word zo- means animal, living being, for example, protozoa, zoo and zoology.

38. C
The stem root word serv- means save, protect, serve, for example conservation.

39. B
The stem root word pre- means before, for example previous.

40. D
The stem root word osteo- means relating to bone, for example osteoporosis.

41. A
The stem root word lacer- means tear, for example laceration.

42. B
The stem root word irat- means anger for example irate.

43. C
The stem root word fin- means relating to end, for example finish and final.

44. A
The stem root word exo- means relating to outside, for ex-

ample exothermic.

45. D
The stem root word verb- means relating to word, for example verbal, verbatim, verbosity.

46. B
The stem root word glob- means relating to sphere, for example global and globule.

47. A
The stem root word athl- means relating to prize, for example athlete, triathlon.

48. C
The stem root word cav- means relating to hollow, for example cave, cavity and excavation.

49. A
The stem root word hygr- means relating to wet, for example hygrometer.

50. D
The stem root word joc- means relating to joke, for example jocularity.

Most Common Prefix

A prefix is a word part at the beginning of a word which helps create the meaning. Understanding prefix is a powerful tool for increasing your vocabulary because many prefix are used by two, three or more words. The word prefix contains a prefix "pre-," which means before. If you know the meaning of the prefix, you can guess the meaning of the word, even if you are not familiar with the word.

Prefix may have more than one meaning. Here is a list of 100 commonly used prefixes along with their meaning and an example of their use.

Study the list below and then answer 50 questions on common prefixes.

Prefix	Meaning	Example
a-, an-	without	amoral
ana-	out of	anachronism
ante-	before	antecedent
acro-	high up	Acropolis
anti-	against	antifreeze
ab-	away	abduction
auto-	self	autopilot
aero-	air	aeroplane
agro-	farming	agriculture
auto-	self	automatic
anti-	against	antidote
anthropo-	human	anthropology
aqua	water	aquarium
bathy-	deep	bathyscape
bio-	life	biology
baro-	atmosphere	barometer
brady-	slow	bradycardia
bi-	two	bicycle
broncho-	breathing	bronchitis
biblio-	relating to books	bibliophile
circum-	around	circumcision
cent- centi-	hundred	centenary

Prefix	Meaning	Example
counter-	against, opposite	counterpoint
cardio-	heart	cardiovascular
cyto-	hollow, receptacle,	cytoplasm
cosmo-		cosmology
cryo-	frost, icy cold	cryogenics
chrono-	time	chronology
com-, con-	together	conference
contra-, contro	against, opposite	contradiction, contraception
crypto-	hidden	cryptography
demo-	people, nation	demographics
dermo-, derma-	skin	dermatology
deci-	one tenth	deciliter
dis-	reverse	dissent
de-	taking away	decentralization
deca	ten	decameter
dynamo-	power, force	dynamic
eco-	house	economy
ectos-	outside	exoskeleton
ex-	out of, former	extract
extra-	more than	extracurricular
hydro	water	hydration
hyper-	over, more	hyperactive
homo-	same	homonym
hetero-	different	heterosexual
hydro	water	hydroplane
hemi	half	hemisphere
intra-	between	intravenous
im-, ir-, il-, in-,	not, without	illegal, inconsiderate,
inter-	between	intersect
in-	into	insert
intra	within	intramural, intranet
intro-	in, into	introspect
kilo-	thousand	kilogram
macro	large	marcoeconomics

Prefix	Meaning	Example
meta-	after, beyond	metacarpal
multi-	many	multimillionaire
mis-	bad, wrong	miscarriage
micro-	small, million	microscope, microgram
mega-, megal-	million, large	megabyte, megaphone
macro-	large	macroeconomics
micro-	one millionth	microgram
mal-	bad	maladjusted
mono-	one	monocle
mini-	small	miniskirt, miniscule
multi	many	multiple, multiplicity
non-	not	nonconformist
non-	not, without	nonentity
neo-	new	Neolithic
omni-	all, every	omniscient
over-	too much	overpopulation
octa	eight	octagon
pre-	before	preview , precedent
penta-	five	pentagon
post-	after	Post-Modern
pro-	in favour of	pro-choice, promotion
pan-	all	pantheon
poly-	many	polygon
quadr-, quart-	four	quadrangle
retro-	backward	retrospect
re-, red-	together	reconnect
re-	again, repeatedly	reflection, reduction
recti-	proper, straight	rectangle, rectify
sub-	under	submarine
semi-	half	semi-automatic , semi-detached
syn-	same time	synchronize
super-	extremely	superhuman
tachy-, tacho-	fast, speed	tachometer
tele-, telo-	long distance	telecommunications, telephoto
trans-	across, beyond	transubstantiation
thermo	heat	thermos

Prefix	Meaning	Example
tri-	three	triangle, tricolor
thermo	heat	thermometer
un-	not, opposite	unconstitutional
uni-	one, single	unification
ultra	beyond	ultraviolet
zoo-	relating to animals	zoology

PREFIX PART I ANSWER SHEET.

	A B C D E		A B C D E
1	○ ○ ○ ○ ○	21	○ ○ ○ ○ ○
2	○ ○ ○ ○ ○	22	○ ○ ○ ○ ○
3	○ ○ ○ ○ ○	23	○ ○ ○ ○ ○
4	○ ○ ○ ○ ○	24	○ ○ ○ ○ ○
5	○ ○ ○ ○ ○	25	○ ○ ○ ○ ○
6	○ ○ ○ ○ ○		
7	○ ○ ○ ○ ○		
8	○ ○ ○ ○ ○		
9	○ ○ ○ ○ ○		
10	○ ○ ○ ○ ○		
11	○ ○ ○ ○ ○		
12	○ ○ ○ ○ ○		
13	○ ○ ○ ○ ○		
14	○ ○ ○ ○ ○		
15	○ ○ ○ ○ ○		
16	○ ○ ○ ○ ○		
17	○ ○ ○ ○ ○		
18	○ ○ ○ ○ ○		
19	○ ○ ○ ○ ○		
20	○ ○ ○ ○ ○		

PREFIX PART II ANSWER SHEET.

	A	B	C	D	E			A	B	C	D	E
1	○	○	○	○	○		21	○	○	○	○	○
2	○	○	○	○	○		22	○	○	○	○	○
3	○	○	○	○	○		23	○	○	○	○	○
4	○	○	○	○	○		24	○	○	○	○	○
5	○	○	○	○	○		25	○	○	○	○	○
6	○	○	○	○	○
7	○	○	○	○	○
8	○	○	○	○	○
9	○	○	○	○	○
10	○	○	○	○	○
11	○	○	○	○	○
12	○	○	○	○	○
13	○	○	○	○	○
14	○	○	○	○	○
15	○	○	○	○	○
16	○	○	○	○	○
17	○	○	○	○	○
18	○	○	○	○	○
19	○	○	○	○	○
20	○	○	○	○	○

Prefix Questions Part I.

1. Choose the prefix that means single or uniform.
   a. Uni-
   b. Epic-
   c. Hydra-
   d. Si-

2. Choose the prefix that means self.
   a. Bi-
   b. Me-
   c. Auto-
   d. Co-

3. Choose the prefix that means half.
   a. Non-
   b. Gra-
   c. Dre-
   d. Hemi-

4. Choose the prefix that means long distance.
   a. Mini-
   b. Tele-
   c. Dis-
   d. Sci-

5. Choose the prefix that means ten.
   a. Deca-
   b. Tri-
   c. Ti-
   d. Bri-

6. Choose the prefix that means straight and proper.

   a. Ultra-

   b. Recti-

   c. Pan-

   d. De-

7. Choose the prefix that means water.

   a. Cent-

   b. Andr-

   c. Uni-

   d. Hydro-

8. Choose the prefix that means time.

   a. Trans-

   b. Inter-

   c. Chrono-

   d. Demo-

9. Choose the prefix that means bad.

   a. Bathy-

   b. Mal-

   c. Re-

   d. Ectos-

10. Choose the prefix that means five.

   a. Fi-

   b. Dynamo-

   c. Post-

   d. Penta-

11. **Choose the prefix that means farming.**
    a. Agro-
    b. Kilo-
    c. Poly-
    d. Contra-

12. **Choose the prefix that means new**.
    a. Andro-
    b. Acro-
    c. Neo-
    d. Mis-

13. **Choose the prefix that means all or every.**
    a. Multi-
    b. Omni-
    c. Creo-
    d. Mal-

14. **Choose the prefix that means after.**
    a. Post-
    b. Acro-
    c. Neo-
    d. Mis-

15. **Choose the prefix that means cold.**
    a. Ex-
    b. Zoo-
    c. Cryo-
    d. Fro-

16. Choose the prefix that means above.
    a. Trans-
    b. Gro-
    c. Epi-
    d. Brady-

17. Choose the prefix that means atmosphere.
    a. Baro-
    b. Cro-
    c. Po-
    d. Ato-

18. Choose the prefix that means at the same time.
    a. Semi-
    b. Syn-
    c. Meta-
    d. Omni-

19. Choose the prefix that means too much.
    a. Plu-
    b. Into-
    c. Nat-
    d. Over-

20. Choose the prefix that means opposite and against.
    a. Contra-
    b. Deg-
    c. Erg-
    d. Re-

21. Choose the prefix that means one millionth.

a. Mil-

b. Non-

c. Micro-

d. Con-

22. Choose the prefix that means wrong or bad.

a. Dis-

b. Demo-

c. Grad-

d. Mis-

23. Choose the prefix that means many.

a. Poly-

b. Pro-

c. Pan-

d. Recti-

24. Choose the prefix that means two.

a. Tri-

b. Bi-

c. Maxi-

d. Dre-

25. Choose the prefix that means before.

a. Anti

b. Tachy-

c. Pre-

d. Quin-

Prefix Questions Part I Answer Key.

1. A
The prefix uni means single and uniform, for example unification.

2. C
The prefix auto means self, for example automatic.

3. D
The prefix hemi means half, for example hemisphere.

4. B
The prefix tele means long distance, for example telecommunication.

5. A
The prefix deca means ten, for example decade.

6. B
The prefix recti means straight and proper, for example rectify.

7. D
The prefix hydro means water, for example hydroplane.

8. C
The prefix chrono means time, for example chronograph.

9. B
The prefix mal means bad, for example maladjusted.

10. D
The prefix penta means five, for example pentagon.

11. A
The prefix agro means farming, for example agronomy.

12. C
The prefix neo means new, for example Neolithic.

13. B
The prefix omni means all or every, for example omniscient.

14. A
The prefix post means after, for example postwar.

15. C
The prefix cryo means icy cold, for example cryogenics.

16. C
The prefix epi means above, for example epitaph.

17. A
The prefix baro means atmosphere, for example barometer.

18. B
The prefix syn means same time, for example synchronize.

19. D
The prefix over means too much, for example overtime.

20. A
The prefix contra means opposite or against, for example contradiction.

21. C
The prefix micro means one millionth, for example microgram.

22. D
The prefix mis means wrong or bad, for example misstep or miscarriage.

23. A
The prefix poly means many, for example polygon.

24. B
The prefix bi means two, for example bicycle.

25. C
The prefix pre means before, for example preview.

Prefix Questions Part II

1. Choose the best meaning of the prefix aqua.

    a. Water

    b. Past

    c. Change

    d. Extreme heat

2. Choose the best meaning of the prefix anti.

    a. Water

    b. Enemies

    c. Against

    d. Missing the mark

3. Choose the best meaning of the prefix bio.

    a. Study

    b. Bible

    c. Animals

    d. Life

4. Choose the best meaning of the prefix circum.

    a. Square shape

    b. Around

    c. Junior in level

    d. Border line

5. Choose the best meaning of the prefix ex.

    a. Excessive

    b. After

    c. Former

    d. Next

6. Choose the best meaning of the prefix thermo.

   a. Long distance

   b. Heat

   c. Hard

   d. Pressure

7. Choose the best meaning of the prefix intra.

   a. Square shape

   b. Between

   c. Round

   d. Border line

8. Choose the best meaning of the prefix kilo.

   a. Thousand

   b. Hundred

   c. Plenty

   d. Extra

9. Choose the best meaning of the prefix multi.

   a. Blood

   b. Severe pain

   c. Narrow

   d. Many

10. Choose the best meaning of the prefix mini.

   a. Harsh

   b. Acute

   c. Small

   d. Larger than normal

11. Choose the best meaning of the prefix octa.

   a. Extreme
   b. Eight
   c. Short
   d. Water animal

12. Choose the best meaning of the prefix pro.

   a. Extremely cold
   b. Before
   c. In favor of
   d. Repeat

13. Choose the best meaning of the prefix quad.

   a. 3-Sided
   b. Four
   c. Five
   d. Many sided

14. Choose the best meaning of the prefix retro.

   a. Related to temperature
   b. Against
   c. Deny
   d. Backward

15. Choose the best meaning of the prefix semi.

   a. Half
   b. Complete
   c. Related to money
   d. Related to weapons

16. **Choose the best meaning of the prefix sub.**
    a. Faster
    b. Smaller
    c. Under
    d. Related to water

17. **Choose the best meaning of the prefix ultra.**
    a. Double
    b. Far beyond
    c. Slow
    d. Related to health

18. **Choose the best meaning of the prefix tri.**
    a. Three
    b. Acrobat
    c. Related to time
    d. Related to air

19. **Choose the best meaning of the prefix un.**
    a. Alone
    b. Together
    c. Opposite
    d. Agreement

20. **Choose the best meaning of the prefix zoo.**
    a. Same time
    b. Relating to animals
    c. Related to the forest
    d. Large house

21. Choose the best meaning of the prefix ante.

    a. Relating to the heart

    b. Relating to food

    c. Male animals

    d. Before or previous

22. Choose the best meaning of the prefix homo.

    a. Same

    b. Red in color

    c. Related to blood

    d. Hard

23. Choose the best meaning of the prefix macro.

    a. Related to economy

    b. Different

    c. Large

    d. Female

Prefix Questions Part II Answer Key.

1. A
The prefix aqua means relating to water, for example, aquarium.

2. C
The prefix anti means against, for example, antichrist.

3. D
The prefix bio means life, for example, biology.

4. B
The prefix circum means around, for example circumference.

5. C
The prefix ex means former or out of, for example extract or ex-president

6. B
The prefix thermo means heat, for example thermostat.

7. B
The prefix intra means between, for example intravenous.

8. A
The prefix kilo means thousand, for example kilogram.

9. D
The prefix multi means many, for example multiple.

10. C
The prefix mini means small, for example miniscule.

11. B
The prefix octa means eight, for example octagon.

12. C
The prefix pro means in favor of, for example promotion.

13. B
The prefix quad means four, for example quadruped, or four legs.

14. D
The prefix retro means backward, for example retrospect.

15. A
The prefix semi means half, for example semi-detached.

16. C
The prefix sub means under, for example submarine.

17. B
The prefix ultra means far beyond, for example ultraviolet.

18. A
The prefix tri means three, for example trilogy.

19. C
The prefix un means opposite and not, for example unconstitutional.

20. B
The prefix zoo means animal, for example zoology.

21. D
The prefix ante means before, for example antecedent.

22. A
The prefix homo means same, for example homosexual.

23. C
The prefix macro mean large, for example macroeconomics.

Most Common Synonyms

Synonyms, like prefix and stem words are a great two-for-one strategy for improving your vocabulary fast. Below is a list of the most common synonyms followed by 30 questions.

Word	Synonym	Synonym
Amazing	Extraordinary	Astonishing
Aggravate	Infuriate	Annoy
Arrogant	Imperious	Disdainful
Answer	Respond	Reply
Antagonist	Enemy	Adversary
Attain	Achieve	Reach
Benevolence	Kindness	Charitable
Berate	Disapprove	Criticize
Beautiful	Gorgeous	Attractive
Big	Gigantic	Enormous
Boisterous	Loud	Rowdy
Boring	Uninteresting	Dull
Budget	Plan	Allot
Contradict	Oppose	Deny
Category	Division	Classification
Complete	Comprehensive	Total
Conspicuous	Prominent	Bold
Catch	Seize	Capture
Chubby	Fat	Plump
Congenial	Pleasant	Friendly
Criticize	Berate	Belittle
Delicious	Delectable	Appetizing
Describe	Portray	Picture
Destroy	Ruin	Wreck
Dwindle	Diminish	Abate
Difference	Contrast	Dissimilarity
Decay	Rot	Decompose
Decent	Pure	Honorable
Decipher	Decode	Decrypt
Eager	Enthusiastic	Willing
Elaborate	Enhance	Explain
Explain	Elaborate	Elucidate

Word	Synonym	Synonym
Enjoy	Relish	Savor
Estimate	Predict	Guess
Eccentric	Weird	Odd
Embezzle	Misappropriate	Steal
Fastidious	Exacting	Particular
Flatter	Praise	Compliment
Fantasy	Imagine	Day dream
Fondle	Caress	Stroke
Furious	Raging	Angry
Good	Sound	Excellent
Genuine	Real	Actual
Gay	Happy	Cheerful
Ghastly	Horrible	Gruesome
Handicap	Disadvantage	Disability
Haughty	Proud	Arrogant
Hypocrisy	Pretense	Duplicity
Humiliate	Shame	Humble
Impregnable	Unconquerable	Indomitable
Interesting	Captivating	Engaging
Illicit	Illegal	Unlawful
Immaterial	Irrelevant	Unimportant
Illustrious	Famous	Noble
Impregnable	Unconquerable	Unbeatable
Incoherent	Jumbled	Confused
Insidious	Deceitful	Duplicitous
Itinerary	Schedule	Route
Intrusive	Invasive	Nosy
Jargon	Slang	Lingo
Jovial	Jolly	Genial
Juvenile	Immature	Adolescent
Justification	Reason	Excuse
Justification	Scoff	Mock
Jostle	Shove	Push
Keep	Hold	Retain
Keen	Sharp	Acute
Keel	Swagger	Reel
Look	Gaze	Inspect
Little	Tiny	Small
Limitation	Constraint	Boundary
Least	Lowest	Minimum
Malice	Bitterness	Spite
Match	Identical	Correspond

Word	Synonym	Synonym
Memorial	Commemorate	Monument
Meager	Bare	Scanty
Momento	Gift	Keepsake
Necessary	Required	Essential
Negotiate	Scheme	Bargain
Novice	Learner	Beginner
Narrate	Disclose	Tell
Negligible	Unimportant	Insignificant
Obstinate	Adamant	Stubborn
Omen	Premonition	Foreboding
Opulence	Abundance	Wealth
Omit	Exclude	Disregard
Perplex	Confuse	Astonish
Parcel	Bundle	Package
Pause	Wait	Break
Plight	Situation	Scenario
Quack	Fake	Charlatan
Quip	Joke	Jest
Renown	Famous	Popular
Radiate	Emanate	Effuse
Run	Accelerate	Dash
Romantic	Amorous	Loving
Rebel	Dissent	Renegade
Reconcile	Harmonize	Conciliate
Render	Give	Present
Sanction	Authorize	Approve
Satisfy	Sate	Gratify
Strong	Powerful	Hard
Sealed	Stroll	Walk
Shackle	Retrain	Confine
Saunter	Shut	Close
Terminate	End	Finish
True	Accurate	Factual
Thrive	Prosper	Progress
Tumult	Confusion	Disturbance
Tacit	Implicit	Implied
Terminate	End	Finish
Thaw	Unfreeze	Defrost
Update	Modernize	Renew
Ultimate	Supreme	Eventual
Uncanny	Mysterious	Spooky
Valid	Accurate	Legitimate

Word	Synonym	Synonym
Verify	Validate	Certify
Vacate	Quit	Resign
Various	Assortment	Diverse
Wrath	Rage	Fury
Weird	Strange	Odd
Yearly	Annually	Year by year
Yank	Pull	Draw
Yearn	Long for	Desire
Zealous	Enthusiastic	Dedicated
Zoom	Speed off	Hurry

SYNONYM PRACTICE QUESTION ANSWER SHEET.

	A	B	C	D	E		A	B	C	D	E
1	○	○	○	○	○	21	○	○	○	○	○
2	○	○	○	○	○	22	○	○	○	○	○
3	○	○	○	○	○	23	○	○	○	○	○
4	○	○	○	○	○	24	○	○	○	○	○
5	○	○	○	○	○	25	○	○	○	○	○
6	○	○	○	○	○						
7	○	○	○	○	○						
8	○	○	○	○	○						
9	○	○	○	○	○						
10	○	○	○	○	○						
11	○	○	○	○	○						
12	○	○	○	○	○						
13	○	○	○	○	○						
14	○	○	○	○	○						
15	○	○	○	○	○						
16	○	○	○	○	○						
17	○	○	○	○	○						
18	○	○	○	○	○						
19	○	○	○	○	○						
20	○	○	○	○	○						

Synonym Practice Questions.

1. Select the synonym of conspicuous.

    a. Important

    b. Prominent

    c. Beautiful

    d. Convincing

2. Select the synonym of benevolence.

    a. Happiness

    b. Courage

    c. Kindness

    d. Loyalty

3. Select the synonym of boisterous.

    a. Loud

    b. Soft

    c. Gentle

    d. Warm

4. Select the synonym of fondle.

    a. Hold

    b. Caress

    c. Throw

    d. Keep

5. Select the synonym of impregnable.

    a. Unconquerable

    b. Impossible

    c. Unlimited

    d. Imperfect

6. Select the synonym of antagonist.

    a. Supporter

    b. Fan

    c. Enemy

    d. Partner

7. Select the synonym of memento.

    a. Monument

    b. Remembrance

    c. Gift

    d. Idea

8. Select the synonym of insidious.

    a. Wise

    b. Brave

    c. Helpful

    d. Deceitful

9. Select the synonym of itinerary.

    a. Schedule

    b. Guidebook

    c. Pass

    d. Diary

10. Select the synonym of illustrious.

    a. Rich

    b. Noble

    c. Gallant

    d. Poor

11. Select the pair below that are synonyms.

    a. Jargon and Slang

    b. Slander and Plagiarism

    c. Devotion and Devout

    d. Current and Outdated

12. Select the pair below that are synonyms.

    a. Render and Give

    b. Recognition and Cognizant

    c. Stem and Root

    d. Adjust and Redo

13. Select the pair below that are synonyms.

    a. Private and Public

    b. Intrusive and Invasive

    c. Mysterious and Unknown

    d. Common and Unique

14. Select the pair below that are synonyms.

    a. Renowned and Popular

    b. Guard and Safe

    c. Aggressive and Shy

    d. Curtail and Avoid

15. Select the pair below that are synonyms.

    a. Brevity and Ambiguous

    b. Fury and Light-hearted

    c. Incoherent and Jumbled

    d. Benign And Malignant

16. Select the pair below that are synonyms.

a. Congenial and Pleasant

b. Distort and Similar

c. Valuable and Rich

d. Asset and Liability

17. Select the pair below that are synonyms.

a. Circumstance and Plan

b. Negotiate and Scheme

c. Ardent and Whimsical

d. Plight and Situation

18. Select the pair below that are synonyms.

a. Berate and Criticize

b. Unspoken and Unknown

c. Tenet and Favor

d. Turf and Seashore

19. Select the pair below that are synonyms.

a. Adequate and Inadequate

b. Sate and Satisfy

c. Sufficient and Lacking

d. Spectator and Teacher

20. Select the pair below that are synonyms.

a. Pensive and Alibi

b. Terminate and End

c. Plot and Point

d. Jaded and Honest

CHOOSE THE SYNONYM OF THE UNDERLINED WORD.

21. I cannot wait to try some of the <u>delectable</u> dishes served in the new restaurant.

    a. Unique

    b. Expensive

    c. New

    d. Delicious

22. Can you <u>describe</u> the character of Juliet in the play?

    a. Report

    b. Portray

    c. State

    d. Draw

23. The soldiers <u>destroyed</u> the rebel's camp.

    a. Ruined

    b. Ended

    c. Fixed

    d. Conquered

24. There is a big <u>difference</u> in Esther Pete's grades.

    a. Complication

    b. Dissimilarity

    c. Minus

    d. Increase

25. I can <u>attain</u> my goals in life when I study hard.

    a. Finish

    b. Forget

    c. Effect

    d. Achieve

26. The lecture was so <u>boring</u> everybody was starting to get sleepy.

    a. Uninteresting

    b. Sensible

    c. Fast

    d. Exciting

27. The <u>eager</u> crowd yelled and cheered for their favorite team during the basketball tournament.

    a. Bored

    b. Uninterested

    c. Angry

    d. Enthusiastic

28. The government is planning to <u>end</u> famine through mass food production.

    a. Close

    b. Avoid

    c. Stop

    d. Start

29. Children enjoy playing in the park with their playmates.

    a. Dislike

    b. Relish

    c. Spend

    d. Uninterested

30. Can you elaborate on the reason behind your tardiness?

    a. Define

    b. Correct

    c. Explain

    d. Interpret

SYNONYM PRACTICE ANSWER KEY

1. B
Conspicuous and prominent are synonyms.

2. C
Benevolence and kindness are synonyms.

3. A
Boisterous and loud are synonyms.

4. B
Fondle and caress are synonyms.

5. A
Impregnable and unconquerable are synonyms.

6. C
Antagonist and enemy are synonyms.

7. C
Memento and gift are synonyms.

8. D
Insidious and deceitful are synonyms.

9. A
Itinerary and schedule are synonyms.

10. B
Illustrious and noble are synonyms.

11. A
Jargon and slang are synonyms.

12. A
Render and give are synonyms.

13. B
Intrusive and invasive are synonyms.

14. A
Renowned and popular are synonyms.

15. C
Incoherent and jumbled are synonyms.

16. A
Congenial and pleasant are synonyms.

17. D
Plight and situation are synonyms.

18. A
Berate and criticize are synonyms.

19. B
Sate and satisfy are synonyms.

20. B
Terminate and end are synonyms.

21. D
Delectable and delicious are synonyms.

22. B
Describe and portray are synonyms.

23. A
Destroy and ruin are synonyms.

24. B
Difference and dissimilarity are synonyms.

25. D
Attain and achieve are synonyms.

26. A
Boring and uninteresting are synonyms.

27. D
Eager and enthusiastic are synonyms.

28. C
End and stop are synonyms.

29. B
Enjoy and relish are synonyms.

30. C
Elaborate and explain are synonyms.

Most Common Antonyms

Antonyms, like synonyms and stems, are a great two-for-one strategy for increasing your vocabulary. Below is a list of the most common antonyms, following by practice questions.

Word	Antonym	Antonym
Abundant	Scarce	Insufficient
Abnormal	Standard	Normal
Advance	Retreat	Recoil
Aimless	Directed	Motivated
Absurd	Sensible	Wise
Authentic	Imitation	Fake
Benevolence	Animosity	Indifference
Bloodless	Sensitive	Feeling
Blissful	Miserable	Sorrowful
Brilliant	Dulled	Dark
Certainty	Uncertainty	Doubtful
Capable	Inept	Incompetent
Cease	Begin	Commence
Charge	Discharge	Exonerate
Cohesive	Weak	Yielding
Console	Aggravate	Annoy
Confused	Enlightened	Attentive
Captivity	Liberty	Freedom
Diligent	Negligent	Languid
Dreadful	Pleasant	Pleasing
Decisive	Procrastinating	Indecisive
Deranged	Sane	Sensible
Disable	Enable	Assist
Discord	Harmony	Cooperation
Disjointed	Connected	Attached
Dogmatic	Flexible	Amenable
Erratic	Consistent	Dependable
Ecstatic	Despaired	Tormented
Eligible	Improper	Unfit
Escalate	Diminish	Decrease
Elusive	Confronting	Attracting
Exhibit	Conceal	Hide
Fidelity	Disloyalty	Infidelity

Word	Antonym	Antonym
Factual	Imprecise	Incorrect
Fearful	Courageous	Brave
Famous	Obscure	Unknown
Gaunt	Plump	Thick
Graceful	Awkward	Careless
Goodness	Meanness	Wickedness
Glamorous	Irritating	Offensive
Hard	Soft	Pliable
Hoarse	Smooth	Pleasing
Hidden	Bare	Exposed
Hearty	Apathetic	Lethargic
Harmful	Harmless	Safe
Harsh	Mild	Gentle
Hero	Villain	Antagonist
Idiotic	Smart	Intelligent
Idle	Busy	Working
Illegal	Lawful	Authorized
Illicit	Legal	Lawful
Illuminate	Obfuscate	Confuse
Immense	Tiny	Small
Intimate	Formal	Unfriendly
Identical	Opposite	Different
Immense	Minute	Tiny
Justice	Lawlessness	Unfairness
Jealous	Content	Trusting
Joyful	Sorrowful	Sad
Jumpy	Composed	Collected
Knack	Inability	Ineptitude
Kill	Create	Bear
Keen	Uninterested	Reluctant
Laughable	Serious	Grave
Latter	Former	First
Legible	Unreadable	Unclear
Literal	Figurative	Metaphorical
Loathe	Love	Like
Legendary	Factual	True
Large	Little	Small
Miserable	Cheerful	Joyful
Moderate	Excessive	Unrestrained
Magical	Boring	Ordinary
Minor	Major	Significant
Myriad	Few	Scant

Word	Antonym	Antonym
Narrow	Broad	Wide
Nasty	Pleasant	Magnificent
Nimble	Awkward	Clumsy
Nutritious	Unhealthy	Unwholesome
Optional	Compulsory	Required
Operational	Inactive	Inoperative
Optimistic	Pessimistic	Doubtful
Ordinary	Abnormal	Uncommon
Pester	Delight	Please
Penalize	Forgive	Reward
Placate	Agitate	Upset
Practical	Unfeasible	Unrealistic
Pensive	Shallow	Ignorant
Queasy	Comfortable	Satisfied
Quietly	Loudly	Audibly
Quirky	Conventional	Normal
Qualified	Unqualified	Incapable
Rapid	Slow	Leisurely
Refuse	Agree	Assent
Reluctant	Enthusiastic	Excited
Romantic	Realistic	Pragmatic
Ridicule	Flatter	Praise
Refresh	Damage	Ruin
Rough	Level	Smooth
Sacrifice	Refuse	Hold
Sadistic	Humane	Kind
Sane	Deranged	Insane
Save	Spend	Splurge
Scarce	Abundant	Plenty
Scorn	Approve	Delight
Scatter	Gather	Collect
Shrink	Expand	Grow
Simple	Complex	Complicated
Stingy	Generous	Bountiful
Sterile	Dirty	Infected
Tedious	Interesting	Exciting
Tactful	Indiscreet	Careless
Tough	Weak	Vulnerable
Transparent	Opaque	Cloudy
Terminate	Initiate	Start
Truth	Lie	Untruth
Understand	Misunderstand	Misinterpret

Word	Antonym	Antonym
Usable	Useless	Unfit
Validate	Veto	Reject
Vanquish	Endorse	Surrender
Vanish	Appear	Materialize
Vicious	Gentle	Nice
Vice	Virtue	Propriety
Villain	Hero	Savior
Vulnerable	Strong	Powerful
Wary	Reckless	Careless
Wasteful	Frugal	Thrifty
Wane	Grow	Increase
Weary	Lively	Energetic
Young	Old	Mature
Yonder	Nearby	Close
Zealous	Lethargic	Unenthusiastic
Zap	Inactive	Dull

Antonym Practice Answer Sheet

	A	B	C	D	E		A	B	C	D	E
1	○	○	○	○	○	21	○	○	○	○	○
2	○	○	○	○	○	22	○	○	○	○	○
3	○	○	○	○	○	23	○	○	○	○	○
4	○	○	○	○	○	24	○	○	○	○	○
5	○	○	○	○	○	25	○	○	○	○	○
6	○	○	○	○	○	26	○	○	○	○	○
7	○	○	○	○	○	27	○	○	○	○	○
8	○	○	○	○	○	28	○	○	○	○	○
9	○	○	○	○	○	29	○	○	○	○	○
10	○	○	○	○	○	30	○	○	○	○	○
11	○	○	○	○	○						
12	○	○	○	○	○						
13	○	○	○	○	○						
14	○	○	○	○	○						
15	○	○	○	○	○						
16	○	○	○	○	○						
17	○	○	○	○	○						
18	○	○	○	○	○						
19	○	○	○	○	○						
20	○	○	○	○	○						

Antonym Practice Questions

1. Choose the antonym pair.

    a. Abundant and Scarce

    b. Several and Plenty

    c. Analysis and Review

    d. Obtrusive and Hierarchical

2. Choose the antonym pair.

    a. Bully and Animal

    b. Teary-eyed and Gentle

    c. Tough and Weak

    d. Strong and Massive

3. Choose the antonym pair.

    a. Illuminate and Obfuscate

    b. Resonance and Significance

    c. Resonate and Justify

    d. Rationalize and Practice

4. Choose the antonym pair.

    a. Simple and Complex

    b. Plain and Plaid

    c. Shy and Sinister

    d. Vibrant and Cheery

5. Choose the antonym pair.

    a. Elevate and Escalate

    b. Exhibit and Conceal

    c. Boast and Brood

    d. Show and Contest

6. Choose the antonym pair.

    a. Strict and Tight

    b. Hurtful and Offensive

    c. Unpleasant and Mean

    d. Stingy and Generous

7. Choose the antonym pair.

    a. New and Torn

    b. Advance and Retreat

    c. Next and Last

    d. Followed and Continued

8. Choose the antonym pair.

    a. Halt and Speed

    b. Began and Amidst

    c. Stop and Delay

    d. Cease and Begin

9. Choose the antonym pair.

    a. Scary and Horrific

    b. Honor and Justice

    c. Immense and Tiny

    d. Vague and Loud

10. Choose the antonym pair.

    a. Dissatisfied and Unsatisfied

    b. Disentangle and Acknowledge

    c. Discord and Harmony

    d. Fruition and Fusion

11. Choose the antonym pair.

    a. Late and Later

    b. Latter and Former

    c. Structure and Organization

    d. Latter and Rushed

12. Choose the antonym pair.

    a. Belittle and Bemuse

    b. Shrunk and Minimal

    c. Shrink and Expand

    d. Smelly and Odor

13. Choose the antonym pair.

    a. Repulsive and Repentant

    b. Reluctant and Enthusiastic

    c. Prepare and Ready

    d. Release and Give

14. Choose the antonym pair.

    a. Sovereign and Autonomy

    b. Disdain and Contempt

    c. Disorder and Disarray

    d. Refuse and Agree

15. Choose the antonym pair.

    a. Gentle and Soft

    b. Fragile and Breakable

    c. Vulnerable and Strong

    d. Vain and Tidy

16. Select the antonym of authentic.

  a. Real

  b. Imitation

  c. Apparition

  d. Dream

17. Select the antonym of villain.

  a. Actor

  b. Actress

  c. Heroine

  d. Hero

18. Select the antonym of vanish.

  a. Appear

  b. Lose

  c. Reflection

  d. Empty

19. Select the antonym of literal.

  a. Manuscript

  b. Writing

  c. Figurative

  d. Untrue

20. Select the antonym of harsh.

  a. Mild

  b. Light

  c. Bulky

  d. Bothersome

21. Select the antonym of splurge.

   a. Spend

   b. Count

   c. Use

   d. Save

22. Select the antonym of idle.

   a. Occupied

   b. Vacant

   c. Busy

   d. Interested

23. Select the antonym of console.

   a. Aggravate

   b. Empathize

   c. Sympathize

   d. Cry

24. Select the antonym of deranged.

   a. Chaos

   b. Dirty

   c. Bleak

   d. Sane

25. Select the antonym of disjointed.

   a. Connected

   b. Dismayed

   c. Recognized

   d. Bountiful

26. Select the antonym of confused.

    a. Frustrated

    b. Ashamed

    c. Enlightened

    d. Unknown

27. Select the antonym of benevolent.

    a. Nice

    b. Mature

    c. Honest

    d. Indifferent

28. Select the antonym of illicit.

    a. Unlawful

    b. Legal

    c. Anonymous

    d. Deceitful

29. Select the antonym of sterile.

    a. Dirty

    b. Alcoholic

    c. Drunk

    d. Drug

30. Select the antonym of myriad.

    a. Many

    b. Several

    c. Few

    d. Plenty

Antonyms Answer Key

1. A
Abundant and scarce are antonyms.

2. C
Tough and weak are antonyms.

3. A
Illuminate and obfuscate are antonyms.

4. A
Simple and complex are antonyms.

5. B
Exhibit and conceal are antonyms.

6. D
Stingy and generous are antonyms.

7. B
Advance and retreat are antonyms.

8. D
Cease and begin are antonyms.

9. C
Immense and tiny are antonyms.

10. C
Discord and harmony are antonyms.

11. B
Latter and former are antonyms.

12. C
Shrink and expand are antonyms.

13. B
Reluctant and enthusiastic are antonyms.

14. D
Refuse and agree are antonyms.

15. C
Vulnerable and strong are antonyms.

16. B
Authentic and imitation are antonyms.

17. D
Villain and hero are antonyms.

18. A
Vanish and appear are antonyms.

19. C
Literal and figurative are antonyms.

20. A
Harsh and mild are antonyms.

21. D
Splurge and save are antonyms.

22. C
Idle and busy are antonyms.

23. A
Console and aggravate are antonyms.

24. D
Deranged and sane are antonyms.

25. A
Disjointed and connected are antonyms.

26. C
Confused and enlightened are antonyms.

27. D
Benevolent and indifferent are antonyms.

28. B
Illicit and legal are antonyms.

29. A
Sterile and dirty are antonyms.

30. C
Myriad and few are antonyms.

How to Prepare for a Test

MOST STUDENTS HIDE THEIR HEADS AND PROCRASTINATE WHEN FACED WITH PREPARING FOR AN EXAM, HOPING THAT SOMEHOW THEY WILL BE SPARED THE AGONY, ESPECIALLY IF IT IS A BIG ONE THAT THEIR FUTURES RELY ON. Avoiding a test is what many students do best and unfortunately, they suffer the consequences because of their lack of preparation.

Test preparation requires strategy and dedication. It is the perfect training ground for a professional life. Besides having several reliable strategies, successful students also has a clear goal and know how to accomplish it. These tried and true concepts have worked well and will make your test preparation easier.

The Study Approach

Take responsibility for your own test preparation.

It is a common - but big - mistake to link your studying to someone else's. Study partners are great, but only if they are reliable. It is your job to be prepared for the test, even if a study partner fails you. Do not allow others to distract you from your goals.

Prioritize the time available to study

When do you learn best, early in the day or at night? Does your mind absorb and retain information most efficiently in small blocks of time, or do you require long stretches to get the most done? It is important to figure out the best blocks of time available to you when you can be the most productive. Try to consolidate activities to allow for longer periods of study time.

Find a quiet place where you will not be disturbed

Do not try to squeeze in quality study time in any old location. Find some place peaceful and with a minimum of distractions, such as the library, a park or even the laundry room. Good lighting is essential and you need to have comfortable seating and a desk surface large enough to hold your materials. It is probably not a great idea to study in your bedroom. You might be distracted by clothes on the floor, a book you have been planning to read, the telephone or something else. Besides, in the middle of studying, that bed will start to look very comfortable. Whatever you do, avoid using the bed as a place to study since you might fall asleep to avoiding studying!

The exception is flashcards. By far the most productive study time is sitting down and studying and studying only. However, with flashcards you can carry them with you and make use of odd moments, like standing in line or waiting for the bus. This isn't as productive, but it really helps and is definitely worth doing.

Determine what you need to study

Gather together your books, your notes, your laptop and any other materials needed to focus on your study for this exam. Ensure you have everything you need so you don't waste time. Remember paper, pencils and erasers, sticky notes, bottled water and a snack. Keep your phone with you if you need it to find essential information, but keep it turned off so others can't distract you.

Have a positive attitude

It is essential that you approach your studies for the test with an attitude that says you will pass it. And pass it with flying colors! This is one of the most important keys to successful studying. Believing that you are capable helps you to become capable.

The Strategy of Studying

Review class notes

Stay on top of class notes and assignments by reviewing them frequently and regularly. Re-writing notes can be a terrific study trick, as it helps lock in information. Pay special attention to any comments that have been made by the teacher. If a study guide has been made available as part of the class materials, use it! It will be a valuable tool to use for studying.

Estimate how much time you will need

If you are concerned about the amount of time you have available it is a good idea to set up a schedule so that you do not get bogged down on one section and end without enough time left to study other things. Remember to schedule break time, and use that time for a little exercise or other stress reducing techniques.

Test yourself to determine your weaknesses

Look online for additional assessment and evaluation tools available for a particular subject. Visit our website http://www.test-preparation.ca for test tips and more practice questions. Once you have determined areas of concern, you will be able to focus on studying the information they contain and just brush up on the other areas of the exam.

Mental Prep – How to Psych Yourself Up for a Test

Since tests are often a big factor in your final grade or acceptance into a program, it is understandable that taking tests can create a great deal of anxiety for many students. Even students who know they have learned the required material find their minds going blank as they stare at the test booklet. One easy way to overcome that anxiety is to prepare mentally for the test. Here are a few simple techniques.

Do not procrastinate

Study the material for the test when it becomes available, and continue to review the material until the test day. By waiting until the last minute and trying to cram for the test the night before, you actually increase anxiety. This leads to an increase in negative self-talk. Telling yourself "I can't learn this. I am going to fail" is a pretty sure indication that you are right. At best, your performance on the test will not be as strong if you have procrastinated instead of studying.

Positive self-talk.

Positive self-talk drowns out negative self-talk and to increases your confidence level. Whenever you begin feeling overwhelmed or anxious about the test, remind yourself that you have studied enough, you know the material and that you will pass the test. Both negative and positive self-talk are really just your fantasy, so why not choose to be a winner?

Do not compare yourself to others.

Do not compare yourself to other students. Instead, focus on your strengths and weaknesses and prepare accordingly. Regardless of how others perform, your performance is the only one that matters to your grade. Comparing yourself to others increases your anxiety and negative self-talk before the test.

Visualize.

Make a mental image of yourself taking the test. You know the answers and feel relaxed. Visualize doing well on the test and having no problems with the material. Visualizations can increase your confidence and decrease the anxiety you might otherwise feel before the test. Instead of thinking of this as a test, see it as an opportunity to demonstrate what you have learned!

Avoid negativity.

Worry is contagious and viral - once it gets started it builds on itself. Cut it off before it gets to be a problem. Even if you are relaxed and confident, being around anxious, worried classmates might cause you to start feeling anxious. Before the test, tune out the fears of classmates. Feeling anxious and worried before an exam is normal, and every student experiences those feelings at some point. But you cannot allow these feelings to interfere with your ability to perform well. Practicing mental preparation techniques and remembering that the test is not the only measure of your academic performance will ease your anxiety and ensure that you perform at your best.

How to Take a Test

EVERYONE KNOWS THAT TAKING AN EXAM IS STRESSFUL, BUT IT DOES NOT HAVE TO BE THAT BAD! There are a few simple things that you can do to increase your score on any type of test. Take a look at these tips and consider how you can incorporate them into your study time.

OK - so you are in the test room - Here is what to do!

Reading the Instructions

This is the most basic point, but one that, surprisingly, many students ignore and it costs big time! Since reading the instructions is one of the most common, and 100% preventable mistakes, we have a whole section just on reading instructions.

Pay close attention to the sample questions. Almost all standardized tests offer sample questions, paired with their correct solutions. Go through these to make sure that you understand what they mean and how they arrived at the correct answer. Do not be afraid to ask the test supervisor for help with a sample that confuses you, or instructions that you are unsure of.

Tips for Reading the Question

We could write pages and pages of tips just on reading the test questions. Here are a few that will help you the most.

- **Think first.** Before you look at the answer, read and think about the question. It is best to try to come up with the correct answer before you look at the options. This way, when the test-writer tries to trick you with a close answer, you will not fall for it.

- **Make it true or false.** If a question confuses you,

then look at each answer option and think of it as a "true" "false" question. Select the one that seems most likely to be "true."

- **Mark the Question.** For some reason, a lot of test-takers are afraid to mark up their test booklet. Unless you are specifically told not to mark in the booklet, you should feel free to use it to your advantage.

- **Circle Key Words.** As you are reading the question, underline or circle key words. This helps you to focus on the most critical information needed to solve the problem. For example, if the question said, "Which of these is not a synonym for huge?" You might circle "not," "synonym" and "huge." That clears away the clutter and lets you focus on what is important.

- **Always underline these words:** all, none, always, never, most, best, true, false and except.

- **Eliminate.** Elimination is the best strategy for multiple choice answers *and* questions. If you are confused by lengthy questions, cross out anything that you think is irrelevant, obviously wrong, or information that you think is offered to distract you.

- **Do not try to read between the lines.** Usually, questions are written to be straightforward, with no deep, underlying meaning. Generally, the simple answer really is the correct answer. Do not over-analyze!

How to Take a Test - The Basics

Some sections of the test are designed to assess your ability to quickly grab the necessary information; this type of exam makes speed a priority. Others are more concerned with your depth of knowledge, and how accurate it is. When you start a new section of the test, look it over to determine whether the test is for speed or accuracy. If the test is for speed (a lot of questions and a short time), your strategy is clear; answer as many questions as quickly as possible.

The MELAB® does NOT penalize for wrong answers, so if all else fails, guess and make sure you answer every question.

Make time your friend

Budget your time from the beginning until you are finished, and stick to it! The amount of time you are permitted for each portion of the test will almost certainly be included in the instructions.

Easy does it

One smart way to tackle a test is to locate the easy questions and answer those first. This is a time-tested strategy that never fails, because it saves you a lot of unnecessary anxiety. First, read the question and decide if you can answer it in less than a minute. If so, complete the question and go to the next one. If not, skip it for now and continue to the next question. By the time you have completed the first pass through this section of the exam, you will have answered a good number of questions. Not only does it boost your confidence, relieve anxiety and kick your memory up a notch, you will know exactly how many questions remain and can allot the rest of your time accordingly. Think of doing the easy questions first as a warm-up!

Do not watch your watch

At best, taking an important exam is an uncomfortable situation. If you are like most people, you might be tempted to subconsciously distract yourself from the task at hand. One of the most common ways to do so is by becoming obsessed with your watch or the wall clock. Do not watch your watch! Take it off and place it on the top corner of your desk, far enough away that you will not be tempted to look at it every two minutes. Better still, turn the watch face away from you. That way, every time you try to sneak a peek, you will be reminded to refocus your attention to the task at hand. Give yourself permission to check your watch or the wall clock after you complete each section. Focus on answering the questions, not on how many minutes have elapsed since you last looked at it.

Divide and conquer

What should you do when you come across a question that is so complicated you may not even be certain what is being asked? As we have suggested, the first time through, skip the question. At some point, you will need to return to it and get it under control. The best way to handle questions that leave you feeling so anxious you can hardly think is by breaking them into manageable pieces. Solving smaller bits is always easier. For complicated questions, divide them into bite-sized pieces and solve these smaller sets separately. Once you understand what the reduced sections are really saying, it will be much easier to put them together and get a handle on the bigger question. This may not work with every question - see below for how to deal with questions you cannot break down.

Reason your way through the toughest questions

If you find that a question is so dense you can't figure out how to break it into smaller pieces, there are a few strategies that might help. First, read the question again and look for hints. Can you re-word the question in one or more different ways? This may give you clues. Look for words that can function as either verbs or nouns, and try to figure out what the questions is asking from the sentence structure. Remember that many nouns in English have several different meanings. While some of those meanings might be related, sometimes they are completely distinct. If reading the sentence one way does not make sense, consider a different definition or meaning for a key word.

The truth is, it is not always necessary to understand a question to arrive at a correct answer! The most successful strategy for multiple choice is Elimination. Frequently, at least one answer is clearly wrong and can be crossed off the list of possible correct answers. Next, look at the remaining answers and eliminate any that are only partially true. You may still have to flat-out guess from time to time, but using the process of elimination will help you make your way to the correct answer more often than not - even when you don't know what the question means!

Do not leave early

Use all the time allotted to you, even if you can't wait to get out of the testing room. Instead, once you have finished, spend the remaining time reviewing your answers. Go back to those questions that were most difficult for you and review your response. Another good way to use this time is to return to multiple-choice questions in which you filled in a bubble. Do a spot check, reviewing every fifth or sixth question to make sure your answer coincides with the bubble you filled in. This is a great way to catch yourself if you made a mistake, skipped a bubble and therefore put all your answers in the wrong bubbles!

Become a super sleuth and look for careless errors. Look for questions that have double negatives or other odd phrasing; they might be an attempt to throw you off. Careless errors on your part might be the result of skimming a question and missing a key word. Words such as "always," "never," "sometimes," "rarely" and the like can give a strong indication of the answer the question is really seeking. Don't throw away points by being careless!

Just as you budgeted time at the beginning of the test to allow for easy and more difficult questions, be sure to budget sufficient time to review your answers. On essay questions and math questions where you are required to show your work, check your writing to make sure it is legible.

Math questions can be especially tricky. The best way to double check math questions is by figuring the answer using a different method, if possible.

Here is another terrific tip. It is likely that no matter how hard you try, you will have a handful of questions you just are not sure of. Keep them in mind as you read through the rest of the test. If you can't answer a question, looking back over the test to find a different question that addresses the same topic might give you clues.

We know that taking the test has been stressful and you can hardly wait to escape. Just keep in mind that leaving before you double-check as much as possible can be a quick trip to disaster. Taking a few extra minutes can make the difference between getting a bad grade and a great one. Besides, there will be lots of time to relax and celebrate after the test is turned in.

In the Test Room – What you MUST do!

If you are like the rest of the world, there is almost nothing you would rather avoid than taking a test. Unfortunately, that is not an option if you want to pass. Rather than suffer, consider a few attitude adjustments that might turn the experience from a horrible one to...well, an interesting one! Take a look at these tips. Simply changing how you perceive the experience can change the experience itself.

You have to take the test - you can't change that. What you can change, and the only thing that you can change, is your attitude -so get a grip - you can do it!

Get in the mood

After weeks of studying, the big day has finally arrived. The worst thing you can do to yourself is arrive at the test site feeling frustrated, worried, and anxious. Keep a check on your emotional state. If your emotions are shaky before a test it can determine how well you do on the test. It is extremely important that you pump yourself up, believe in yourself, and use that confidence to get in the mood!

Don't fight reality

Students often resent tests, and with good reason. After all, many people do not test well, and they know the grade they

How to Take a Test

end with does not accurately reflect their true knowledge. It is easy to feel resentful because tests classify students and create categories that just don't seem fair. Face it: Students who are great at rote memorization and not that good at actually analyzing material often score higher than those who might be more creative thinkers and balk at simply memorizing cold, hard facts. It may not be fair, but there it is anyway. Conformity is an asset on tests, and creativity is often a liability. There is no point in wasting time or energy being upset about this reality. Your first step is to accept the reality and get used to it. You will get higher marks when you realize tests do count and that you must give them your best effort. Think about your future and the career that is easier to achieve if you have consistently earned high grades. Avoid negative energy and focus on anything that lifts your enthusiasm and increases your motivation.

Get there early enough to relax

If you are wound up, tense, scared, anxious, or feeling rushed, it will cost you. Get to the exam room early and relax before you go in. This way, when the exam starts, you are comfortable and ready to apply yourself. Of course, you do not want to arrive so early that you are the only one there. That will not help you relax; it will only give you too much time to sit there, worry and get wound up all over again.

If you can, visit the room where you will be taking your exam a few days ahead of time. Having a visual image of the room can be surprisingly calming, because it takes away one of the big 'unknowns'. Not only that, but once you have visited, you know how to get there and will not be worried about getting lost. Furthermore, driving to the test site once lets you know how much time you need to allow for the trip. That means three potential stressors have been eliminated all at once.

Get it down on paper

One advantage of arriving early is that it allows you time to recreate notes. If you spend a lot of time worrying about whether you will be able to remember information like names, dates, places, and mathematical formulas, there is a solution for that. Unless the exam you are taking allows you to use your books and notes, (and very few do) you will have to rely on memory. Arriving early gives to time to tap into your memory and jot down key pieces of information you know that will be asked. Just make certain you are allowed to make notes once you are in the testing site; not all locations will permit it. Once you get your test, on a small piece of paper write down everything you are afraid you will forget. It will take a minute or two but by dumping your worries onto the page you have effectively eliminated a certain amount of anxiety and driven off the panic you feel.

Get comfortable in your chair

Here is a clever technique that releases physical stress and helps you get comfortable, even relaxed in your body. You will tense and hold each of your muscles for just a few seconds. The trick is, you must tense them hard for the technique to work. You might want to practice this technique a few times at home; you do not want an unfamiliar technique to add to your stress just before a test, after all! Once you are at the test site, this exercise can always be done in the rest room or another quiet location.

Start with the muscles in your face then work down your body. Tense, squeeze and hold the muscles for a moment or two. Notice the feel of every muscle as you go down your body. Scowl to tense your forehead, pull in your chin to tense your neck. Squeeze your shoulders down to tense your back. Pull in your stomach all the way back to your ribs, make your lower back tight then stretch your fingers. Tense your leg muscles and calves then stretch your feet and your toes. You should be as stiff as a board throughout your entire body.

Now relax your muscles in reverse starting with your toes. Notice how all the muscles feel as you relax them one by one. Once you have released a muscle or set of muscles, allow them to remain relaxed as you proceed up your body. Focus on how you are feeling as all the tension leaves. Start breathing deeply when you get to your chest muscles. By the time you have found your chair, you will be so relaxed it will feel like bliss!

Fight distraction

A lucky few are able to focus deeply when taking an important examination, but most people are easily distracted, probably because they would rather be any place else! There are a number of things you can do to protect yourself from distraction.

Stay away from windows.

If you select a seat near a window you may end gazing out at the landscape instead of paying attention to the work at hand. Furthermore, any sign of human activity, from a single individual walking by to a couple having an argument or exchanging a kiss will draw your attention away from your important work. What goes on outside should not be allowed to distract you.

Choose a seat away from the aisle so you do not become distracted by people who leave early. People who leave the exam room early are often the ones who fail. Do not compare your time to theirs.

Of course, you love your friends; that's why they are your friends! In the test room, however, they should become complete strangers inside your mind. Forget they are there. The first step is to physically distance yourself from friends or classmates. That way, you will not be tempted to glance at them to see how they are doing, and there will be no chance of eye contact that could either distract you or even lead to an accusation of cheating. Furthermore, if they are feeling stressed because they did not spend the focused time studying that you did, their anxiety is less likely to permeate your hard-earned calm.

Of course, you will want to choose a seat where there is sufficient light. Nothing is worse than trying to take an important examination under flickering lights or dim bulbs.

Ask the instructor or exam proctor to close the door if there is a lot of noise outside. If the instructor or proctor is unable to do so, block out the noise as best you can. Do not let anything disturb you.

The MELAB® does not allow any personal items in the exam

room. Eat protein, complex carbohydrates and a little fat to keep you feeling full and to supercharge your energy. Nothing is worse than a sudden drop in blood sugar during an exam.

Do not allow yourself to become distracted by being too cold or hot. Regardless of the weather outside, carry a sweater, scarf or jacket if the air conditioning at the test site is set too high, or the heat set too low. By the same token, dress in layers so that you are prepared for a range of temperatures.

Watch Caffeine

Drinking a gallon of coffee or gulping a few energy drinks might seem like a great idea, but it is, in fact, a very bad one. Caffeine, pep pills or other artificial sources of energy are more likely to leave you feeling rushed and ragged. Your brain might be clicking along, all right, but chances are good it is not clicking along on the right track! Furthermore, drinking lots of coffee or energy drinks will mean frequent trips to the rest room. This will cut into the time you should be spending answering questions and is a distraction in itself, since each time you need to leave the room you lose focus. Pep pills will only make it harder for you to think straight when solving complicated problems on the exam.

At the same time, if anxiety is your problem try to find ways around using tranquilizers during test-taking time. Even medically prescribed anti-anxiety medication can make you less alert and even decrease your motivation. Being motivated is what you need to get you through an exam. If your anxiety is so bad that it threatens to interfere with your ability to take an exam, speak to your doctor and ask for documentation. Many testing sites will allow non-distracting test rooms, extended testing time and other accommodations as long as a doctor's note that explains the situation is made available.

Keep Breathing

It might not make a lot of sense, but when people become anxious, tense, or scared, their breathing becomes shallow and, in some cases, they stop breathing all together! Pay attention to your emotions, and when you are feeling worried, focus on your breathing. Take a moment to remind yourself to breathe deeply and regularly. Drawing in steady, deep breaths energizes the body. When you continue to breathe deeply you will notice you exhale all the tension.

It is a smart idea to rehearse breathing at home. With continued practice of this relaxation technique, you will begin to know the muscles that tense up under pressure. Call these your "signal muscles." These are the ones that will speak to you first, begging you to relax. Take the time to listen to those muscles and do as they ask. With just a little breathing practice, you will get into the habit of checking yourself regularly and when you realize you are tense, relaxation will become second nature.

Avoid Anxiety Before a Test

Manage your time effectively

This is a key to your success! You need blocks of uninterrupted time to study all the pertinent material. Creating and maintaining a schedule will help keep you on track, and will remind family members and friends that you are not available. Under no circumstances should you change your blocks of study time to accommodate someone else, or cancel a study session to do something more fun. Do not interfere with your study time for any reason!

Relax

Use whatever works best for you to relieve stress. Some folks like a good, calming stretch with yoga, others find expressing themselves through journaling to be useful. Some hit the floor for a series of crunches or planks, and still others take a slow stroll around the garden. Integrate a little relaxation time into your schedule, and treat that time, too, as sacred.

Eat healthy

Instead of reaching for the chips and chocolate, fresh fruits and vegetables are not only yummy but offer nutritional benefits that help to relieve stress. Some foods accelerate stress instead of reducing it and should be avoided. Foods that add to higher anxiety include artificial sweeteners, candy and other sugary foods, carbonated sodas, chips, chocolate, eggs, fried foods, junk foods, processed foods, red meat, and other foods containing preservatives or heavy spices. Instead, eat a bowl of berries and some yogurt!

Get plenty of ZZZZZZZs

Do not cram or try to do an all-nighter. If you created a study schedule at the beginning, and if you have stuck with that schedule, have confidence! Staying up too late trying to cram in last-minute bits of information is going to leave you exhausted the next day. Besides, whatever new information you cram in will only displace all the important ideas you've spent weeks learning. Remember: You need to be alert and fully functional the day of the exam

Have confidence in yourself!

Everyone experiences some anxiety when taking a test, but exhibiting a positive attitude banishes anxiety and fills you with the knowledge you really do know what you need to know. This is your opportunity to show how well prepared you are. Go for it!

Do not chitchat with friends

Let your friends know ahead of time that it is not anything personal, but you are going to ignore them in the test room! You need to find a seat away from doors and windows, one that has good lighting, and get comfortable. If other students are worried their anxiety could be detrimental to you; of course, you do not have to tell your friends that. If you are afraid they will be offended, tell them you are protecting them from your anxiety!

Common Test-Taking Mistakes

Taking a test is not much fun at best. When you take a test and make a stupid mistake that negatively affects your grade, it is natural to be very upset, especially when it is something that could have been easily avoided. So what are some of the common mistakes that are made on tests?

Do not fail to put your name on the test

How could you possibly forget to put your name on a test? You would be amazed at how often that happens. Very often, tests without names are thrown out immediately, resulting in a failing grade.

Marking the wrong multiple-choice answer

It is important to work at a steady pace, but that does not mean bolting through the questions. Be sure the answer you are marking is the one you mean to. If the bubble you need to fill in or the answer you need to circle is 'C', do not allow yourself to get distracted and select 'B' instead.

Answering a question twice

Some multiple-choice test questions have two very similar answers. If you are in too much of a hurry, you might select them both. Remember that only one answer is correct, so if you choose more than one, you have automatically failed that question.

Mishandling a difficult question

We recommend skipping difficult questions and returning to them later, but beware! First, be certain that you do return to the question. Circling the entire passage or placing a large question mark beside it will help you spot it when you are reviewing your test. Secondly, if you are not careful to skip the question, you can mess yourself up badly. Imagine that a question is too difficult and you decide to save it for later.

You read the next question, which you know the answer to, and you fill in that answer. You continue to the end of the test then return to the difficult question only to discover you didn't actually skip it! Instead, you inserted the answer to the following question in the spot reserved for the harder one, thus throwing off the remainder of your test!

Incorrectly Transferring an answer from scratch paper

This can happen easily if you are trying to hurry! Double check any answer you have figured out on scratch paper, and make sure what you have written on the test itself is an exact match!

Thinking too much

Oftentimes, your first thought is your best thought. If you worry yourself into insecurity, your self-doubts can trick you into choosing an incorrect answer when your first impulse was the right one!

Conclusion

CONGRATULATIONS! You have made it this far because you have applied yourself diligently to practicing for the exam and no doubt improved your potential score considerably! Passing your up-coming exam is a huge step in a journey that might be challenging at times but will be many times more rewarding and fulfilling. That is why being prepared is so important.

Study then Practice and then Succeed!

Good Luck!

Thanks!

If you enjoyed this book and would like to order additional copies for yourself or for friends, please check with your local bookstore, favorite online bookseller or visit www.test-preparation.ca and place your order directly with the publisher.

Feedback to the author may be sent by email to feedback@test-preparation.ca

Visit Us Online

Taking a test? We can help!

Complete study guides, practice test questions, study tips and more: www.test-preparation.ca

Endnotes

Reading comprehension passages where noted below are used under the Creative Commons Attribution-ShareAlike 3.0 License. For details visit,

http://en.wikipedia.org/wiki/Wikipedia:Text_of_Creative_Commons_Attribution-ShareAlike_3.0_Unported_License

[1] What is Free Range Chicken In *Answers.com*. Retrieved Feb 14, 2009, from http://wiki.answers.com/Q/What_is_free-range_chicken.

[2] Grizzly Bear. In *Wikipedia*. Retrieved Feb 14, 2009, from http://en.wikipedia.org/wiki/Grizzly_Bear.

[3] Grizzly Polar Bear Hybrid. In *Wikipedia*. Retrieved Feb 14, 2009, from http://en.wikipedia.org/wiki/Grizzly%E2%80%93polar_bear_hybrid.

[4] Peafowl. In *Wikipedia*. Retrieved Feb 14, 2009, from en.wikipedia.org/wiki/Peafowl.

[5] Smallpox. In *Wikipedia*. Retrieved Feb 14, 2009, from http://en.wikipedia.org/wiki/Smallpox.

[6] Lightning. In *Wikipedia*. Retrieved Feb 14, 2009, from http://en.wikipedia.org/wiki/Lightning.

[7] Venus. In *Wikipedia*. Retrieved Feb 14, 2009, from http://en.wikipedia.org/wiki/Venus.

[8] Weather. In *Wikipedia*. Retrieved Feb 14, 2009, from http://en.wikipedia.org/wiki/Weather.

[9] Ebola Virus. In *Wikipedia*. Retrieved May 9, 2012, from en.wikipedia.org/wiki/Ebola_virus_disease.

[10] Megabat. In *Wikipedia*. Retrieved May 2012, from http://en.wikipedia.org/wiki/Megabat

[11] List of Greek and Latin Roots in English. In *Wikipedia*. Retrieved Feb 14, 2009, from http://en.wikipedia.org/wiki/List_of_Greek_and_Latin_roots_in_English.

[12] *Wiktionary*. Retrieved Feb 14, 2009, from http://en.wiktionary.org/wiki/.

[13] Infectious Disease. In *Wikipedia*. Retrieved Feb 14, 2009, from http://en.wikipedia.org/wiki/Infectious_disease.

[14] Virus. In *Wikipedia*. Retrieved Feb 14, 2009, from http://en.wikipedia.org/wiki/Virus.
[15] Outline of Meteorology. In *Wikipedia*. Retrieved Feb 14, 2009, from http://en.wikipedia.org/wiki/Outline_of_meteorology.
[16] Butterfly. In *Wikipedia*. Retrieved Feb 14, 2009, from http://http://en.wikipedia.org/wiki/Butterfly.
[17] United States Navy SEALs. In *Wikipedia*. Retrieved Feb 14, 2009, from http://en.wikipedia.org/wiki/United_States_Navy_SEALs.